Bruce Larson

NO LONGER STRANGERS

Books by Bruce Larson

The One and Only You
Ask Me to Dance
No Longer Strangers
Thirty Days to a New You
Living on the Growing Edge
Setting Men Free
Dare to Live Now
The Edge of Adventure (with Keith Miller)
Living the Adventure (with Keith Miller)
The Emerging Church (with Ralph Osborne)
There's a Lot More to Health Than Not Being Sick
Risky Christianity
The Whole Christian
Wind and Fire
The Communicator's Commentary: Luke

Bruce Larson

NO LONGER STRANGERS

WORD BOOKS
PUBLISHER
WACO, TEXAS

A DIVISION OF
WORD, INCORPORATED

Library of Congress Catalog Card Number 74-146675

No Longer Strangers by Bruce Larson. Copyright
© 1971, 1985 by Word, Incorporated, Waco, Texas 76703.

Scripture quotations from the *Revised Standard
Version of the Bible* are used by permission of the
Division of Christian Education, National Council
of Churches in the United States of America.
Quotations from *The New Testament in Modern
English* by J. B. Phillips, copyright © J. B. Phillips,
1958 are used by permission of The
Macmillan Company.
The poem "Earth" is reprinted by permission of
Charles Scribner's Sons from *The Gardener and Other
Poems* by John Hall Wheelock. Copyright
© 1961, John Hall Wheelock.

Printed in the United States of America

This book is dedicated to my parents,
who first introduced me to the mysteries
and complexities of relationships,
and to all the people mentioned in this book,
from whom I have learned so much.

Contents

Introduction

My wife and I are the parents of three children, all now adults, and two of them are themselves parents. My highest goal for my children and grandchildren alike is that they might know God and live the life of faith. I find myself eagerly anticipating the day when my grandchildren might ask the question, "What does it really mean to be a Christian?" I don't know of any simple way to answer that question, but I have been thinking about it for a long time, and this book contains what I would say if I were given the opportunity and sufficient time to explore the question at length.

Of course I realize that the answer I would give today to such a question is not the answer I might give a few years from now. Because of new insights gained and new experiences lived through, modifications are certain to take place. But at this point in my life, this book is an honest attempt to outline my answer to the hypothetical question—whether or not it is ever asked!

What does it really mean to be a Christian?

Obviously, one can answer immediately that to be a Christian is to know Jesus Christ as your Lord and Savior. But to explain what *that* means requires a good deal, as any honest and realistic person knows. Man's nature and man's needs may remain the same from age to age, but changes are taking place perpetually in the Church and in the world, and a good answer must take such changes into account.

Moreover, a person's answer also grows out of his own autobiography or spiritual pilgrimage. Otherwise it is incomplete and somewhat hypocritical, if it relies on theories or doctrines which are automatically accepted, or on half-hearted convictions.

This book—my "answer"—must therefore be unashamedly personal. It is also, I hope, unashamedly biblical. But it is something else, as well: an attempt to interpret some of the fantastic changes that are taking place both in the Church and in the world—changes that many Christians find threatening.

My starting point is the word "gospel," which means, literally, "good news." The gospel is Jesus Christ Himself, the incarnation of God's love and our living, contemporary Lord. Having said that, one must immediately grapple with the question it raises: Why is Jesus Christ such good news?

At this point in my life there is a text that sums up for me the tremendous mystery and wonder of why the gospel is still good news. In the Revised Standard Version of the Bible, Ephesians 2:19 reads this way:

"So then you are no longer strangers and sojourners, but you are fellow citizens with the saints and members of the household of God."

To me, the gospel is good news right now because in Jesus Christ we find a God who deals with perhaps the most oppressive and pervasive problem of our time—the problem of estrangement and loneliness.

I am convinced that this problem of loneliness and separation is the underlying cause behind the destructive behavior everywhere evident in our world; behavior which we could not ignore even if we wanted to because it is splashed across the front pages of our daily newspapers and relentlessly reiterated on our television screens. War, drug addiction, confrontation, alcoholism, suicide, exploitation, sexual excesses and perversions, physical and political repression—surely these aggressions and escape mechanisms are man's imperfect ways of dealing with this basic problem of loneliness and estrangement. If man were truly integrated—at one with himself, with his fellows, and with his world—would there be chaos of such alarming proportions?

In Jesus Christ, the living Lord, we find the only means I know of to deal with this deep estrangement, this perennial human problem. That is why today, as in every age, the gospel is the best of news for every man, whatever his intellect or emotional makeup or theological persuasion or philosophy or station in life. If we could understand what God has done and what He offers in Jesus Christ, we would be like David the king, dancing before the Ark of the Lord, celebrating the great good news of God's grace and His offer of inclusion in the household of God as well as in the household of man.

It is this good news that transcends the multitude of changes taking place in the world and in the Church, changes that baffle and confuse not only the young but even the mature. The permanence of Jesus Christ lies in the nature of His permanent answer to life's most baffling problem— not in some new ecclesiasticism or theology or legalism or ethical code.

Does this mean that there are no absolutes in life? I don't think so. The Ten Commandments, for example, I believe to be absolutes. But it does mean that man in his insecurity attempts to make absolutes of many things that were not intended to be so. And when these things crumble and change, man's world seems to be threatened.

Change, of course, has always been the rule rather than the exception. But in other times changes came more slowly and were therefore less threatening; things had the appearance of being orderly and static. Today we live in an age when the rate of change has been accelerated in nearly every dimension of life, creating the impression of chaos and inducing panic in the hearts of men and women.

Recently I came across a document listing the entrance requirements for South Hadley Seminary (now Mount Holyoke College). Here are some of the standards which the founders of that school considered adequate for young women who applied for admission in its early days:

1. Admission. No young lady shall become a member of this school who cannot kindle a fire, wash potatoes, and repeat the multiplication table.
2. Outfit. No cosmetics, perfumeries, or fancy soaps will be allowed on the premises.
3. Exercise. Every member of this school shall walk at least a mile every day unless a freshet, earthquake, or some other calamity prevents.
4. Company. No member of this school is expected to have any male acquaintances unless they are retired missionaries or agents of some benevolent society.
5. Times at the mirror. No member of this institution shall tarry before the mirror more than three consecutive minutes.
6. Reading. No member of this school shall devote more than one hour each week to miscellaneous reading. "The Atlantic Monthly," Shakespeare, Scott's novels, *Robinson Crusoe,* and immoral works are strictly forbidden. "The Boston Recorder," "Missionary Herald," and Washington's Farewell Address are earnestly recommended for light reading.

Such a list gives us a view of the Christian life and ethic which seems absurdly outdated to us today, and yet we react defensively to any suggestion by today's young people that our present Christian views and ethics are also seriously outdated.

I vividly recall seeing a young man some years ago at a Christian rally who was toting a sign that read, "Jesus, Yes. Christianity, No."

This is typical of the emphasis among many young people who are serious about Jesus Christ. They say that to be a Christian today does not mean that we have to defend two thousand years of Christianity, including countless examples of inhumanity, repression, and brutality as well as tremendous positive achievements. Youth today feel free to discover what it means to be a disciple of Jesus Christ.

This is, I believe, a liberating rather than a chaotic development. It does not throw out the marvelous heritage of these two thousand years, but it certainly liberates us from having to defend a great deal of misguided zeal, as well as the physical and political and social persecutions that have gone on under the guise of Christianity. In a positive sense, this freedom can be a basis for discovering once again why the gospel is good news.

There is one further point I would like to make by way of introduction: a distinction which I believe to be biblical but which I am sure will disturb some readers.

I see a distinction between living a "Christian life" and living life as a Christian.

To imply that there is some standard look or manner or personality or behavior that we can call "Christian" can be a most binding, defeating, and destructive assumption. On the other hand, to realize that God has not only made allowance for the uniqueness of personality but has actually initiated it, making every person unique, sheds an entirely different light on what the gospel is all about.

One of the things I have sought to do in this book is to explore the fact that Jesus Christ calls us *in our uniqueness* to belong not only to the Father and to Him, but also to one another in this fellowship called the Church.

He calls us from our isolation and loneliness and efforts to conform— efforts that must end in failure—to the point where we bring our emerging uniqueness to the Father and to one another and are made one. We are "no longer strangers." Not because we all look alike, sound alike, or smell alike, but because we have heard the good news, dropped our defenses, and dared to move into the dance of life. The movement is not away from God and ourselves and one another, but into ever-diminishing concentric circles with God at the corner.

One further point: I frequently use the word "man" in this book. Please note that it is used, along with the appropriate pronouns which follow it, in the primary, the so-called generic, sense of the term, to mean the human race at its most inclusive or the human race simply as such.

Relational Theology—
The Missing Ingredient

When we operate within a framework of a relational theology, we see that the good news is relevant in two dimensions. First, there is the fact that in Jesus Christ we need no longer be strangers but can belong to a community of people who are seeking a birthright, a home, and relationships through God's love and grace. This changes our goals. We are not trying to make people believe "the right things" so much as enabling them to experience a relationship with God and with one another. Second, our ministry becomes different. We are no longer teachers, but those who through the rediscovery of the principles of relational theology enter into relationship with others and bring them to life.

1

The Missing Ingredient

The Bible is primarily a book of stories, stories of God interacting with His people, and it deals only indirectly with doctrine. Despite that fact, throughout the history of the church and up to the present day, a great deal more time has been spent on digging into doctrinal aspects of the faith than on exploring its relational aspects. One has only to look into the issues considered in theological seminaries and in the councils of the church to recognize that this is so.

At the heart of the gospel is the good news that God became man in Jesus Christ. Our faith rests not in disembodied concepts but in a personal God revealed in scripture. We can have a relationship with that personal God, and that primary relationship affects all other relationships. It seems to me our "orthodoxy" ought to have as much to do with the quality of those relationships than with our doctrinal stands.

Life's problems are usually relational, even though they may stem from ideological or doctrinal differences. Perhaps this explains why most of us find modern novelists much more relevant to real issues than most preachers. A good novelist probes the forces that lead us to destroy one another, to become contentious, withdrawn, aloof, hostile, critical and violent. Too many preachers, on the other hand, fall into the trap of dealing theoretically with doctrinal and ethical problems.

If the Christian message is to make a significant impact on the affairs of our time, it certainly must deal with the forces, causes and motives that divide individuals and nations, as well as with those forces that draw us together, enable relationships and bring healing and reconciliation. We may very well eventually destroy our own world (this is itself a theological and doctrinal question!) but such a catastrophe will not be primarily because of differing ideologies but because of irreconcilable relationships under the respectable cover of doctrinal disagreements.

John Hall Wheelock calls attention to this fact in his poem, "Earth":

"A planet doesn't explode of itself," said drily
The Martian astronomer gazing off into the air.
"That they were able to do it is proof that highly
Intelligent beings must have been living there."*

Our comic strip artists often speak pertinently to the human predicament in terms of our relationships. For example, in a typical "Blondie" strip we find Mr. Dithers, Dagwood's boss, coming into the office saying, "Cora and I had an awful argument this morning." Trying to comfort him, Dagwood asks, "What was it all about?" Mr. Dithers replies, "That's what made it so aggravating—we couldn't think of a subject!" We laugh and yet we realize the cartoonist has portrayed the nature of life and the flavor of hell, lostness, and estrangement in terms that anyone can understand. And the Christian message speaks precisely to this condition. Very simply, God became flesh and lived among us in Jesus Christ and died and was raised from the dead so that a man and his wife would not have to destroy a marriage with irrelevant arguments— and so that man would not have to blow up his world for reasons irrelevant or otherwise. Jesus Christ came to enable relationships that bring people closer to one another and closer to God.

Sound doctrine is, of course, important, but it does little in itself to enable relationships. Certainly it helps to understand clearly the nature of God, of sin and grace, but knowledge and understanding do not necessarily change behavior or enable life.

The truth of that struck me with fresh impact some years ago when my oldest son was a teenager. Peter had the privilege of spending ten

---

*John Hall Wheelock, *The Gardener and Other Poems* (New York: Charles Scribner's Sons).

days at a Young Life ranch. When he returned, I met his bus and immediately noticed a difference in this "typical" adolescent boy. He was outside himself, communicative, sensitive and excited.

As we drove home, the first thing Peter said gave me a clue not only to what had happened but to how it had happened. "Dad," he said, "I became a Christian at the ranch last week. It's strange: I didn't learn a thing about Jesus that I didn't know before I went there. But I met some people who were real."

This boy of mine has always been something of a theologian and has lived in the realm of ideas. He has grasped doctrinal principles from a very early age. I could well believe that it was not his knowledge of doctrine that had been enlarged at the ranch. Rather, he had spent time with leaders who knew how to live out life with people in such a way that God could break through and begin to transform.

It seems to me that if the church is to come alive in our day, it must discover this dimension of ministry where life is laid down alongside life in such a way that a teenager or a senior citizen can discover the grace of God and begin to experience the miracle of new life as my son did.

That such an important dimension of truth should have escaped us for so long is surprising. But it should not be, because it can happen—and has happened—in other disciplines.

For example, surgeons of a century ago killed most of their patients. No one seemed to know why. One can imagine a conscientious surgeon going back to medical school for further training, determined to find out whether he had lost or forgotten some basic technique, desperate to improve his skill. After further refining his technique and absorbing still more theory, he would return to his practice—and still kill most of his patients.

Then along came a doctor who had a theory about germs. He suggested that all doctors wash their hands before performing surgery. The idea was not readily accepted. As a matter of fact, this visionary doctor was subjected to such ridicule and humiliation that he died in a mental hospital.

Eventually, however, his ideas caught hold and doctors began to practice antiseptic surgery. The rest is history. Surgical techniques are still being refined and elaborated, to the benefit of all of us who are patients, but there is no question that it was the added dimension of antisepsis which was crucial.

This is precisely what I suggest for present-day theology. We need doctrine; we need to define it, refine it, and examine it constantly in the light of the Bible and in the light of the wisdom God is revealing through other disciplines. But it is impotent if its implications do not have relational application.

Without this, we may go on preaching doctrinal truths and "killing the patients." "The letter killeth, but the Spirit giveth life." There are underlying principles that God has revealed in Scripture and continues to reveal in daily life that show us how we can cooperate with Him in the releasing of life, the healing of relationships, the liberation of people and the reconciliation that is so desperately needed in our time. We can discover these principles together.

The organization known as Alcoholics Anonymous practices a relational theology. Members of AA have a strategy of loving and caring for one another that has brought sobriety to thousands of desperate drunks. And most pastors, faced with the task of helping an alcoholic, recommend that he join AA, knowing he will find more help there than in a good many churches, however sound doctrinally. AA, though doctrinally questionable by Christian standards, is relationally sound. The church ought to be both!

The Church of Christ ought to be a fellowship of people who are doctrinally sound and relationally whole. When these dimensions of the faith are both taken seriously, we can expect a rebirth of life in the church. And this is exactly what is happening in scattered churches across the nation. New life is emerging because the personal and relational dimensions of the faith are being discovered, explored and applied.

J. B. Phillips gives us a helpful translation of Romans 12:19: "Let there be no imitation Christian love among you." This seems to me an accurate translation of what Paul wrote. He did not say that there are imitation Christians so much as that genuine Christians can love in an imitation way. How do we love genuinely in relationships as we attempt to cooperate with God in His plans to transform life and liberate people? Let me list some of the things I think we need to do:

1. *Identify*

I believe we ought to come alongside those in need and discover with them the adequacy of Christ. The temptation is to identify ourselves with God and try to speak for Him and to bring His help to others. Our

motives may be perfectly genuine and sincere, but sometimes our attitude implies that we no longer have any problems. The other person
perceives that he or she is a "project," and we all resist being someone
else's project. On the other hand, if we identify with those people we are
trying to help, which is easy to do if we are at all honest, then together
we can lay hold on Christ's power to transform life.

2. Include

One important leadership principle is that people support only that
which they help to create. This explains why so many church programs
die aborning. What often happens is that the minister or the church
officers go off and prayerfully consider what program to present to the
congregation for the coming year. They consider priorities, formulate a
program, and offer it as a package to the rest of the church. When the
response is less than enthusiastic, and those programs are not supported
with leadership, money, and prayers, the architects feel that the members are reactionary, stingy, uncommitted, unconverted, or hard of heart.

But this may not be the case at all. It may simply be that all of us have
a built-in resistance to ideas and plans which we have not helped to
develop. The officers need to include the church at large in the planning
stage. The congregation could be marshalled into small groups to discuss
and recommend agenda items for the annual meeting, and to balance
priorities and make program proposals. The membership as a whole
might come up with the very same program that the ministers or officers
tried to force upon them—or they might propose an even better one.

The significant difference between the two approaches is that in the
second church members have discovered the thrill of being partners with
God in finding the priorities that are in His mind for the local church.
This approach reflects a sound doctrinal interpretation concerning the
Holy Spirit and how He operates. In his sermon at Pentecost, the apostle
Peter reminded his hearers of the prophecy that "in the latter days" God
would put His Spirit into all men and that all should dream dreams and
see visions.

It seems to me this shared-leadership approach is distinctively New
Testament in its characteristics. In the Old Testament, one man—like
Moses or one of the prophets—went off to commune with God and
returned to present His plans and pronouncements to the Israelites. But
the Old Testament records indicate this method failed repeatedly. When

the people were confronted with the will of God on a "take it or leave it" basis, more often than not they left it. Or if they initially accepted it, the falling away began almost immediately.

In the New Covenant, God has given His Holy Spirit to all of His people. When we take this promise seriously, we can rely on the whole family of God for wisdom and leadership, and together we will accept priorities and build agendas for redemptive, cooperative ministries.

3. Encourage

We need, more and more, to help laymen and women discover that they are God's primary agents to change and transform the world and to bring in His kingdom. This is an insight to which most of us clergymen are blind. As a result, we have a hard time in training and equipping the laity for ministry. The role of the clergyman in this area is to help men and women discover that they have gifts for ministry, and to call forth those gifts.

In terms of the lay apostolate, we see a natural and inevitable progression: having discovered their own gifts and ministries, these lay apostles in turn become those who can approach their peers in business, schools and neighborhoods and help others recognize and call forth the gifts God has given them.

This single insight is at the heart of the grass roots renewal taking place in parishes across the country today. It changes our whole approach to ministry, from the point of view of either clergy or laity. Ministry is shared. The priesthood of all believers is a reality.

4. Embrace

In terms of the nature of the church in this latter half of the twentieth century, we need more and more to embrace the lost, the disenfranchised, the helpless. The church is for losers. The church is not for those who "have it made" or for those who are an entrenched part of the "establishment," however you choose to interpret or identify the establishment. Yes, the church is for the dispossessed and for those who can honestly say that they do not have it made.

The condition of our world today underlines how relevant this rediscovery is. Our world is no longer being shaped by geopolitical forces but by psychopolitical forces. Consider the kinship felt and expressed by people in various groups who feel cheated, left out, exploited, and powerless. The restless, frustrated minorities of America, black, hispanic or whatever, feel at one not with those of their race who have it made economically and socially, but with those who are also seeking a distinct identity, recognition and power: the migrant worker who has been mercilessly shortchanged and exploited; the Eskimo who has the misfortune to live on top of a vast oil field; the woman who considers her status in society to be definitely second-class; the Indian who is systematically excluded from the mainstream of life; or the teenager who has purchasing power but no political power.

Another phenomenon of our time is the emergence of "ethnic blocks": Italian Americans, for example, and Polish Americans and others who feel that they have been ignored and discriminated against. Within a few short years American society has been fragmented and polarized to a truly frightening extent.

But if we are honest we will realize that even those in places of power can identify in their inmost beings with the "losers" and the second-class. No one totally has it made.

Where the church has been identified solely with those who are "at one with God" and therefore at one with the establishment—the forces for preserving the status quo—it has become irrelevant. But where the church can unashamedly be made up of a fellowship of those who do not have it made, who are looking for more in life either emotionally, politically, financially, or socially, it speaks a relevant word to man and is true to its New Testament calling.

In Jesus Christ we need no longer be strangers but can belong to a community of people who are seeking a birthright, a home, and relationships through God's love and grace. This changes our goals. We are not trying to make people believe "the right things" so much as enabling them to experience a relationship with God and with one another. And those relationships with one another ought to be marked, as we have said, by identification, inclusion, encouragement and a love that embraces.

Our ministry is to relate in redemptive ways, even as Jesus Christ related to us by His incarnation, death, and resurrection, and by His Holy Spirit becomes available to us now as the indwelling presence.

Communication
Is the Problem

It is truly exciting to see how God, the great communicator, is trying to teach His people new ways to listen to Him and new ways to communicate one with another so that we may no longer be strangers.

2

Communication
Is the Problem

If the name of the game is relationships, then it's no wonder that our main problem is that of communication.

Someone has observed that the Kingdom of God is the kingdom of right relationships. There is much wisdom in this observation, and it immediately reminds us that in order to have right relationship, the greatest tool or asset we can have is the ability to communicate.

To be in a right relationship with God, one must be able to communicate with Him—able to speak to God with assurance and to hear what He says in return. To have a good relationship with oneself, one must be able to hear that "inner voice" and to tell oneself the truth about one's own desires, yearnings, needs, hopes, and fears. And to have a good relationship with one's fellowman means that a person must be able to maintain adequate two-way communication: speaking in such a way that others hear what is being said, and listening in such a way that one hears accurately what the other is saying.

Scripture sheds a bright light on the communication problem, for the entire Bible can be seen as an exposition of the theme of communication throughout the history of God's dealing with His creatures and our dealing with ourselves and with those around us.

The very first chapters of Genesis describe how God initiates a relationship with us that is both a verbal and a nonverbal acting out of "I love you." Love implies trust, and God asks us to respond to His love in trust. But the Genesis account makes clear that at the very outset of history, man was either unable or unwilling to hear God, defied the relationship of trust, and broke communication.

Following the break, we see God trying to reestablish the relationship. "Where are you?" He asks Adam. Adam is hiding behind the bushes, acting out his response by concealing himself. Of course, concealment always breaks down communication.

The story of the second generation of man reiterates and strengthens this theme. After Cain kills Abel, God again tries to establish relationship and begins with some simple communication. "Where is your brother?" He asks Cain.

Knowing full well where his brother is, Cain replies evasively, "How do I know? Am I my brother's keeper?"

Again the problem is one of communication. The problem is not that God is unwilling to become involved with man or to have a relationship with him or to speak clearly to him, but that man is both unwilling and unable to extricate himself from the lies and deviousness and disobedience that make him deliberately break the relationship and feign the inability to communicate.

Perhaps nothing indicates more of the nature of God's fantastic love for man than His repeated willingness—in biblical history and in current events—to establish communication with man. Biblical insights and personal experience both underline the fact that man continually rebuffs this attempt on God's part and pretends deafness or ignorance.

A clear example of this is found in the story of Moses. Moses breaks through into a relationship with God whereby the two can speak person to person. Coming down from the mountain, he tells the people of Israel what God is trying to say to them, and then invites them to climb the mountain to hear God speak.

Their response is deeply interesting and profoundly sad. In effect, they say, "No. You go up and speak with God and tell us what He has to say." The reason for their response is obvious. If people hear what God says through the lips of a human being, they can always question the validity and integrity of that person. If they hear God speak for themselves, they have no recourse but to obey or to defy God openly. I believe this problem persists in the Church today. People would rather listen to the preacher telling them what God is saying than initiate a life of devotion where they would meet Him face to face and hear His personal word for them. One source is easy to discount; the other must be reckoned with.

This problem of communication undermines not only the relationship between God and man but also between man and his fellows. Listen to conversation between lovers, parents, friends, colleagues, or strangers and you will sense something of the dilemma psychologists have been probing for decades: the programmed indifference by which we do not even hear one another. In his poem, "Two Friends," David Ignatow states the problem starkly:

I have something to tell you.
  I am listening.
I am dying.
  I am sorry to hear.
I am growing old.
  Terrible.
It is. I thought you should know.
  Of course. I'm sorry. Keep in touch.
You too.
  And let me know what's new.
Certainly. Though it can't be much.
  And stay well.
And you too.
  And go slow.
And you too.*

Part of the problem is that we are conditioned early in life to be either verbal or nonverbal, either givers or receivers in a relationship. We are not born with equal facility in all categories. Part of our redemption consists of the fact that God makes us whole people, endows the listeners with the ability to speak and the talkers with the ability to listen. He makes those who are basically givers able to become receivers, and those who enjoy receiving able to give—not only gifts but themselves.

"Fiddler on the Roof" † is a marvelous musical play that ran on Broadway for years. Few plays have spoken so deeply to me about the nature of the divine-human comedy.

---

*Steven Dunning (et. al, eds.), *Some Haystacks Don't Even Have Any Needle*, Poem quoted, "Two Friends" by David Ignatow (New York: Lothrop, Lee and Shepard Co., Inc.).

† Joseph Stein et. al, *Fiddler on the Roof* (New York: Crown Publishers, Inc.)

Tevye, the main character in the play, is a middle-aged Jewish peasant living in a small, out-of-the-way Russian village toward the end of the nineteenth century. He has discovered something of the grace of God and the marvelous plan God has for every man, and his whole life has become a prayer: a two-way communication with God. Tevye turns to God with all his complaints: about the Russians, about his family, about business, about crops. At one point he says, "God, you say money is a curse. So curse me, just once, just a little bit!"

Life for this Jewish peasant is a struggle, and his relationship with God does not shield him from troubles and tragedies. For one thing, his three older daughters all make disastrous marriages—from Tevye's point of view.

During the course of the play there is a poignant scene when, without any warning, this funny, common, little man turns to his equally struggling and hard-pressed wife and asks, "Do you love me?"

She turns and says, "Do I love you! What a question!" Who, she asks, has been preparing his food, washing his clothes, scrubbing his floors, tending his garden, sharing his bed, and raising his children all these years?

But her response fails to satisfy Tevye. Again he asks, "But do you love me?" and again she mentions all the things she has done for him throughout their married life. Again he presses her with the question, "Do you love me?" And still she cannot answer in any way but to point to her faithfulness as a wife.

Here is an illustration of the tragedy of sin. Sin is not made up only of hostile acts or overt crimes—robbing a bank, getting drunk, or committing adultery. Sin is being unable to hear the person God has put next to you in life who is saying something to you in a way different from what you are "programmed" to hear. And somehow you pass each other like two ships in the night.

Of course Tevye's wife loves him, but he wants her to say so (as most of us men do who are hopeless romantics). And he loves her, but she wants him to act out his love in a thousand little gestures that spell concern and caring.

Well, the acting out is not quite enough for him, and the words are not quite enough for her, and there we see in a single dramatic scene the essence of the tragedy of life and marriage.

The remedy lies in Jesus Christ. When He enters the picture, romance can be established or reborn in two people who live together, though one is verbal and the other nonverbal; though one is a giver and the other a receiver.

Most of us tend to be drawn to our opposites, so this becomes a picture of most marriages. And apart from God making each of us new by His own grace, marriage often ends up as an armed truce or perhaps a semi-tragedy.

During a workshop my wife and I once led on "Family Life," one of the men in attendance volunteered that he would like to report on an experiment he and his wife had begun about ten months before.

Their problem, as he described it, was that he was unable to tell his wife his deepest fears, longings, sins, and mistakes because whenever he spoke deeply about himself he saw a look of censure on her face. The wife's problem with her husband was similar: each time she would try to express what she was truly like inside, her husband appeared to be bored or indifferent or disgusted.

They were about to consult a marriage counselor when they hit on an experiment. They bought two tape recorders, one for him and one for her.

His work involved traveling a good deal of the time, and he would take his tape recorder along in the car or on the plane. When his wife was not physically present and he could not see her face, he was able to pour out all of himself to her on tape. When her husband was away, the wife would tape record her messages to him, expressing herself freely.

Then, of course, they would exchange the tapes and when they were again separated he would listen to his wife as he traveled, and she at home would listen to him revealing his innermost thoughts and desires.

They reported to our workshop that a new relationship of intimacy had been found as a result of this experiment.

I couldn't resist asking if they had tried speaking to each other directly without tape recorders. "Oh, no," was the response, "we've tried that and it still doesn't work!"

We all laughed, and yet we believed that God had started this couple on a new redemptive program and that they would eventually get beyond the gimmick stage into direct dialogue. But how marvelous that these two did not settle for something less than honest communication! They knew that God had a better plan for them than the placid but only semi-satisfying marriage they had experienced during their first years together.

The need for deep, honest communication is obviously not confined to married couples. It is crucial for parents and children, and extremely important also for friends, co-workers, and fellow church members.

There are times when a gimmick—such as a tape recorder or a small group situation—will enable people to begin to open up to one another. But in any event, God's ultimate will is that people learn to speak face to face in open communication and to discover that by the grace of God they need no longer be strangers.

As Christians, we have been notoriously bad at hearing one another. One of our dodges has been to focus on "saving souls" while forgetting that souls are people. Ernest L. Stech states the problem succinctly in his poem, "That's My Soul."

That's my soul lying there.

You don't know what a soul is?
You think it's some kind of ghostly sheetlike thing you can see through and
    it floats in the air?
That's my soul lying there.

Remember when my hand shook because I was nervous in the group?
Remember the night I goofed and argued too much and got mad and couldn't
    get out of the whole mess?
I was putting my soul on the line.
Another time I said that someone once told me something about herself that
    she didn't have to.
I said that she told me something that could have hurt her.
And I guess I was asking you to do the same.
I was asking you to let me know you.
That's part of my soul, too.

When I told you that my mother didn't love my dad and I knew it as a kid,
When I said that my eyes water when I get hurt even though I'm thirty-four
    and too much a man to cry,
I was putting my soul out there in the space between you and me.
Yeah, that's my soul lying there.

I've never met God.
I mean I've never met that old man who sits on a cloud with a crown and a
    staff and knows everything and is everything and controls everything.
But I've met you.

Is that God in your face?
Is that God in your soul lying there?

Well, that's my soul lying there.
I'll let you pick it up.
That's why I put it there.

It'll bruise and turn rancid like an old banana if you want to manhandle it.
It'll go away if you want to ignore it.

But if you want to put your soul there beside it, there may be love.
There may even be God.

Jesus Christ died to save men and women in their totality, not just their souls. As a matter of fact, the Hebrew word translated into English as "soul" has to do with the very life of man. When we in the church relate to a person, we need to relate to the whole person and to hear all that he or she is saying. Moreover, we need to reveal all of ourselves that we are able to reveal at the time—to let the other person know all of us. In this way we begin to discover something of the kingdom of right relationships, which is one description of the Kingdom of God.

Merely trying to "save souls" in the usual sense of the term is like playing tennis against a wall: you bounce the ball against the wall and it returns at an equal or opposite angle—but you are not playing a real game; you are simply playing with yourself. This is what I think Martin Buber meant when he talked about "I-thou" as contrasted to "I-it." When we speak of souls, we usually think of *its*. But when we think of a person, we think of another one like ourselves.

Jesus Christ is such another one. He comes from God to have a relationship with us whereby we can truly speak and truly listen. He also reminds us that we cannot relate to Him without relating to one another. This is what the Church is all about. It is people hearing one another and trying to reveal as much of themselves as they can in an act of total love, even as Jesus Christ revealed all of Himself.

Probing the nature of God and people through a rediscovery of relational theology, we are finding new things about communication. We find that communication employs not only our words, but also the symbols we use and the secret signals we send to one another.

An experience I had on a plane some years ago focused my attention on this whole matter of communication and taught me a good deal about establishing right relationships. I was flying from Pittsburgh to Dayton, Ohio, with a friend. The plane was nearly empty, and as we moved to the rear to take our seats, one of the stewardesses caught sight of my tie clasp and exclaimed, "You're wearing keys!"

"Yes," I said.

"They're papal keys," she added.

I had not thought of that, but not wanting to be caught off guard I replied, "Yes, they are.'

"What do they mean?" she asked rather suspiciously.

"Well," I said, "I believe that every Christian holds in his hands the keys to the Kingdom of God. Jesus said that those whom we let in come in, and those whom we keep out by our words or attitudes or relationships, stay out."

Instantly the stewardess brightened. "I believe that, too," she said. "I'm an underground Catholic. My friend over here is an underground Methodist."

You can imagine how my friend and I responded to this news. No sooner was the plane aloft and the other passengers settled than the two attendants came back and the four of us had a "small group meeting" all the way to Dayton.

We soon discovered that these two young women, who lived in San Francisco, were looking for some lively church contacts there. We suggested some names and then went on to share with them news of vital Christians like themselves in places like Dayton and New York, as well as San Francisco.

Later, in thinking over this encounter, I began to wonder what would have happened if I had been wearing a more traditional symbol, such as a cross in my lapel. Or if I had been carrying a Bible in my hand. Perhaps these might have elicited the same response, but frankly I doubt it.

I also began to think about the apparent contradiction in Jesus' two commandments that we are to be His witnesses and that we are to fish for people. If we really understood, I suppose there would be no contradiction. But on the surface, at least, there are apparently two kinds of Christians: "establishment" and "underground." In the first century all Christians were misunderstood and persecuted and had to resort to using secret identifying symbols.

But the question for all of us Christians—whether we regard ourselves as part of the establishment or the underground—is this: What are we trying to communicate to others by what we say or wear or do? It is not enough to wear some traditional symbol of the faith. Our intention may be good, but the person on the receiving end may misunderstand completely.

A parallel to this situation may be seen in the current use of the American flag, displayed by many in front of their homes or as appendages to their automobiles or as lapel buttons. In theory there is nothing wrong with a person displaying a flag if he loves his country and its symbols. But what does it say to equally patriotic citizens who do not choose to display the flag? Russell Baker, a columnist for *The New York Times*, has suggested that what the flag now says is, "I am a better American than you!" How sad that the American flag, once a symbol around which our citizens could rally, has become instead a sign of division and discord.

The lesson for us Christians is this: We must be aware that communication is a two-way street and that what we intend to say may not be the thing that is heard or "read" by another. After reading Russell Baker's column on the flag, it occurred to me that I am a little wary of the person who wears a cross in his or her lapel. I don't doubt their faith or sincerity or intention; I suspect that I am put off because of inner forces within me that have to do with "one-upsmanship."

What do we mean to say when we wear a cross or carry a Bible or fly a flag? Is it: "Look, I am one with you. I am your friend. Trust me; count on me."? Or is it: "See my symbol? Now you know where I stand, so you'd better watch what you say and do!"

One day on a trip from New York to Texas I tried an experiment in communication-by-signal. It happened that I had to catch a pre-breakfast flight, and because of a number of circumstances and pressures I was well aware that one of the gifts of the Holy Spirit was temporarily missing from my life: the gift of joy. Feeling resentful and out of sorts, I thought of a lapel button that had been given to me some weeks before. The button said simply, "Joy."

In my state of mind, which was anything but joyful, it occurred to me that it might be a good thing to wear that button, expressing what I knew God wanted to give me but which I did not possess at the moment. So I put the Joy button in my lapel and started for the airport.

When I arrived in Austin three planes and two changes later, not only had my own gift of joy been received once again from God, but the button had elicited some marvelous respones from all kinds of people in airports and on the planes. It is very easy when someone asks why you are wearing a button that says Joy to mention that it is one of the most delightful of qualities, and that it comes from God.

Again I asked myself whether there would have been the same kind of response if I had been wearing a cross. Would there have been dozens of people giving me a word of greeting or a smile?

There is a creative kind of communication that we can discover as we live out our faith in the world. Those of us who choose to wear an identifying symbol should make sure that it is not something to make us feel secure, something to hide behind. Rather, it should be a vehicle for initiating conversations, responses, and relationships.

I suppose that what I am trying to say is that our best communication is oblique, for the most part. Direct confrontation often intimidates the receiver. Oblique communication leaves the door open for someone to respond, and for the initiator to identify with his audience.

I once had a most uplifting experience—at a funeral, of all places. It was a funeral for my old friend, Harry. To begin with, the service was conducted by a layman, an artist named Bob Arnold—a fact which underlined the importance of the lay apostolate. At the close of the service, Bob mentioned that Harry had for years attended a men's lunch meeting, and at the close of those meetings the leader would invariably ask, "Does anyone have a 'quickie' before we go?" So Bob asked if anyone had a "quickie" before we closed the funeral service. This provided an opportunity for several friends to stand up and spontaneously talk about Harry, about Jesus Christ, and about how Christ had blessed them over the years through Harry.

It strikes me that anyone attending that service would have caught something of the lay apostolate, the Body of Christ, and the Kingdom of God. In a subtle and beautiful way, the lay ministry and the ministry of witness were taking place before our eyes. The purpose of the funeral was not to provide an occasion for a witness meeting, but to do the thing which came naturally in honoring Harry and his memory and in worshiping God at this time of transition for his family. But the witness was powerful because it came across obliquely.

There was something of the unexpected and surprising in it; something that caught us off guard and spoke powerfully to us of the nature of God and His intentions for His people. True, it would have been natural and sincere of us to show the grief we felt at having to go on without Harry's presence among us—the expected, conventional response. But the nature of this unique funeral service communicated something equally real and far more important. In a curious way, I saw a direct parallel in this experience to the difference between wearing a Joy button and brandishing a Bible.

I want very much to be the kind of Christian who communicates positively and meaningfully to others the style of life I have discovered in Jesus Christ. To do this more effectively, I have been setting some guidelines for myself.

In general, I will not identify myself in a way that tends to intimidate others, for that is leading from strength, not from weakness. Rather, I will try in the months ahead to let myself be guided by these principles:

1. The words I speak or the symbol I wear should convey the fact that I care for the other person. If Jesus Christ lives in me, I should be known as a caring person.

2. What I say or do should communicate something of the fruits of the Spirit in me, such as love or joy or peace. When and if these qualities are perceived, people will be curious about their source.

3. I must give the impression that I identify with the person who meets me. I believe that Jesus always identified with people, and if He lives in me I should try to do the same.

4. My words or the "signals" I transmit should say something about my belief in the other person's potential. Implicit in my attitude should be the conviction that the other person is capable of having what I have, doing what I do, or being what I am in Jesus Christ.

5. Whatever I do or say or whatever symbol I wear should honor the individuality of the person with whom I come in contact. As a Christian I should express the fact that I believe in each person's uniqueness. Rather than attempting to pressure someone else into joining my cause, I need to convey my hope that the other person will find a way to do his or her own thing with God's help.

It is truly exciting to see how God, the great communicator, is trying to teach His people new ways to listen to Him and new ways to communicate one with another so that we may no longer be strangers.

The New Goal . . .
A Christian Style

Christians are not meant to take the place of the Holy Spirit and become super-detectives, ferreting out people's sins and weaknesses and underscoring them. When we employ this kind of strategy, it is no wonder people fail to discover the grace of God in and through us.

Our task as Christians is far easier, more exciting, and more rewarding than that. It is to live out a style of life that will allow people to discover their worth, their strengths, and their uniqueness, and to communicate how much God intends to do with them and for them.

3

The New Goal . . .
A Christian Style

My convictions about a Christian lifestyle were really focused for me in a conversation with my son while he was still a teen-ager. I had stepped into his room to borrow some typing paper. As I was about to leave, he said, "Dad, can I talk to you for a minute?" His tone of voice made me sense that this was going to be something important, and it was.

"Since I became a Christian," Peter said, "I have really been serious about my discipleship."

I knew this was true.

"Almost every morning I've been keeping a quiet time before school, reading my Bible and praying."

This was news to me—the kind of news that truly warms a father's heart.

"But at school during the day," he continued, "what concerns me is how I know whether I am obedient to Jesus Christ. What does it mean to be obedient? It bothers me not to know whether I'm doing what God wants. And I know I don't make much of an impression on anybody else when it comes to faith."

I said I thought he was talking about what constitutes an authentic Christian style of life, and I was able to share with Pete my own convictions.

A Christian style of life ought to be something that is pleasing to God and liberating for other people who come in contact with us. I told Pete that it seemed to me such a style could be boiled down to two simple principles: accepting the love Jesus demonstrated when He gave Himself on the cross for us; practicing His commandment to love one another as He has loved us.

These two ingredients of Christ's love are summed up for me in the words *affirmation* and *vulnerability*.

In the cross Jesus affirms us in that He gives Himself to us as we are. By this He makes clear that we have worth and significance and that He wants us to be a part of God's plan and purpose and to share in God's own love.

The cross also demonstrates that Christ chose to be vulnerable. He did not shield or defend Himself against the laughter, humiliation, and indignity of an unfair trial, nor did He seek to escape physical pain and ultimate crucifixion. Perhaps He was most vulnerable at the point of being abandoned by His closest friends and disciples.

Peter and I talked that day about this kind of love, love which affirms others and their worth and is at the same time vulnerable to them. Love like this is not easy. It takes the power of the Holy Spirit living in us to achieve it. "But with these two guidelines," I said to my son, "I can measure in any situation or any relationship at any given time the degree of my own obedience and the quality of my Christian style of life."

I remember that a long conversation followed about what affirmation and personal vulnerability might look like in a classroom or on the playing field or in a friendship or a dating situation. Every situation is different, and yet the two principles always apply and give us some guidelines of what it means to obey Jesus and to love one another as He loved us.

Earlier in this book we touched on the centrality of communication to right relationships. At this point we must go a step further and declare that communication is not enough. It is possible for us to be in good communication with those around us and yet totally ineffective or irrelevant to them. The necessary added dimension is, of course, the Christian style.

A bizarre illustration of how one can be in communication and yet totally ineffective was given to me by a medical doctor, an eye, ear, nose, and throat specialist. During the course of our conversation he told of having attended a meeting some years before, a dinner meeting during a medical convention. About seventy doctors were present, all specialists in the same field.

In the midst of the banquet, one of the doctors got a fishbone stuck in his throat and began to choke. Virtually every person in the room grasped the situation at once—was in full communication with the suffering colleague. What is more, any one of them could probably have saved his life by performing an emergency tracheotomy. But as they cast about helplessly for a tool that might be used to make the necessary incision, their colleague died.

The doctor concluded his story by saying that ever since that night he had carried a scalpel in his pocket so that he would be prepared for just such an emergency. He added that a lot of the other doctors present at that dinner now did the same thing.

This story made me think of the parallel situation in the Christian life. One may have learned the secret of communication and become able to diagnose the needs of those with whom he interacts, and yet remain irrelevant and helpless because he does not have the tools necessary to deal with those needs. Having the right tools makes it possible for one to be a link between God's power and the needs of people. The ingredients of a Christian style of life provide those essential tools. Jesus Christ had them and used them. His command that we love one another as He loved us means, I believe, that we too can do the same.

What a delightful experience it is to find oneself on the receiving end of the ministry of affirmation! I had an experience like that some years ago. Even today, the memory of it has the power to lift my spirits and turn me "from death to life."

Early one morning I had to catch a plane from Newark, New Jersey, to Syracuse, New York, having returned late the previous night from leading one conference and on my way to another.

I was tired. I had not budgeted my time wisely and I was totally unprepared for the intense schedule before me. After rising early and hastily eating breakfast, I drove to the airport in a mood which was anything but positive. By the time the plane took off I felt so sorry for myself, and so guilty because I was unprepared, that I hated God and myself and the people who had invited me to come lead this conference on "renewal." For some of us, unfortunately, such an attitude is not unusual.

Sitting on the plane with an open notebook in my lap, I prayed, "O God, help me. Let me get something down here that will be useful to your people in Syracuse."

Nothing came. I jotted down phrases at random, feeling worse by the moment, and more and more guilty. Such a situation is a form of temporary insanity. It denies all that we know about God Himself and His ability to redeem any situation.

About halfway through the brief flight, a stewardess came down the aisle passing out coffee. All the passengers were men, as women have too much sense to fly at seven o'clock in the morning. As the flight attendant approached my seat, I heard her exclaim, "Hey! Someone is wearing English Leather after shave lotion. I can't resist a man who uses English Leather. Who is it?"

Eagerly I waved my hand and announced, "It's me."

The stewardess immediately came over and sniffed my cheek, while I sat basking in this sudden attention. All through the remainder of the flight the stewardess and I maintained a cheerful banter each time she passed my seat. She would make some comment and I would respond jovially. Twenty-five minutes later when the plane prepared to land I realized that my temporary insanity had vanished. Despite the fact that I had failed in every way—in budgeting my time, in preparation, in attitude—everything had changed. I was freshly aware that I loved God and that He loved me in spite of my failure.

What is more, I loved myself and the people around me and the people who were waiting for me in Syracuse. I was like the Gadarene demoniac after Jesus had touched him: clothed, in my right mind, and seated at the feet of Jesus. I looked down at the notebook in my lap and found a page full of ideas that could prove useful throughout the weekend.

"God," I mused, "how did this happen?" It was then that I realized that someone had entered my life and turned a key. It was just a small key, turned by a very unlikely person. But that simple act of affirmation, that undeserved and unexpected attention, had got me back into the stream of the Holy Spirit and transformed me from someone in a deep depression into a sane, mature Christian.

Afterward I wondered what would have happened if, instead of the stewardess, one of my super-serious Christian friends had encountered me on that flight, and in my imagination I constructed the scene.

Seeing my depression and despair, he or she might have said, "Bruce, you certainly weren't very wise, and you weren't a good steward of your time or your health. And I think your attitude is dreadful." That's just the sort of approach I would have used myself at various times in the past.

Immediately on the defensive, I would have said, "You don't know how hard I work to serve the Lord." And I would have gone on to explain that it really wasn't my fault but the fault of my crowded schedule.

Happily, this scene was all in my mind. The truth is that when I was at my worst, a word of affirmation came that reversed the pattern, changed my direction, and allowed God to draw me out of my sickness.

This hints at the amazing power of affirmation. It is a small measure of what we experience when we see God's love for us in Jesus Christ. While we are at our worst and most rebellious, Christ comes and loves us and gives Himself to us and dies for us.

This power breaks down our defenses, enables us to admit our guilt, and frees us to relax and let God renew our minds and set our feelings right.

How often we Christians have assumed that our job is to underscore other people's problems, sins, and mistakes! If we really believe in the Holy Spirit and the work which God has said He would do in every heart, then we know that our job is not to criticize. It is God who lets people know where they are wrong and where they need to change. Because of the work of the Holy Spirit, every man in his heart knows something of his lacks and failures.

More often, what people do not know is that they have worth and that God loves them as they are; that He can take them in any condition and begin to make them creative, sane, and helpful.

A new breed of Christian is arising in our time, made up of individuals and groups who are discovering the authentic, biblical nature of the ministry of affirmation. It is true that we have all sinned; we are all basically guilty, but when we are criticized, we become defensive and miss out on the ministry of confession. On the other hand, when we are affirmed, we relax enough to admit the nature of our needs and the extent of our wrongs. We can then stand for a moment in the presence of God's love as it comes through another individual.

Christians are not meant to take the place of the Holy Spirit and become super-detectives, ferreting out people's sins and weaknesses and underscoring them. When we employ this kind of strategy, it is no wonder we block God's grace working in and through us.

Our task as Christians is far easier, more exciting, and more rewarding than that. It is to live out a style of life that will allow those around us to discover their worth, their strengths, and their uniqueness, and to communicate how much God intends to do with them and for them.

An unloving, unresponsive spouse does not need to be reminded of his or her failure. Children who are failing in school do not need to be told that they are lazy or indifferent or goofing off. An employee who cannot do the job does not need to be lectured at every turn that he or she is not measuring up to expectations. A minister who cannot be an adequate shepherd for the congregation does not have to be advised of his or her shortcomings in this area.

All of us know our failures. Tell people that they are failing and they will only get worse. But if you can find and reinforce something positive that God has put in them, they will respond to that, even as we respond to God when He tells us of His love for us in Jesus Christ.

Ever since I saw the musical play, "Man of LaMancha,"* my patron saint has been Don Quixote. This play is based on the theme of Cervantes' monumental novel. It is the story of a senile old man who sets off to do battle with evil in the world. Hundreds of years after the death of chivalry, he dons a rusty suit of armor and goes forth to right wrongs.

His companion is a fat, funny little fellow named Sancho Panza. To Don Quixote, Sancho Panza is the squire of a great knight. Knowing that he is only a humble servant on the old man's farm, Sancho Panza nevertheless loves his master and enters into his fantasy. And so the two set off on their quest: Don Quixote on a spavined horse and Sancho Panza on a mule.

The two ride up to a broken-down inn where mule traders stop. When Don Quixote meets the slovenly innkeeper of this very questionable establishment—which is no Howard Johnson's Motor Lodge—he kneels before him and says something like: "Behold, you are the lord of this great manor. I ask you to knight me in the proper fashion." The innkeeper protests this obvious madness but the Don insists.

At dinner with the mule traders, Don Quixote sees the poor, misused kitchen wench who comes in to serve the meal. In his eyes she is a pure and beautiful maiden, Dulcinea, and he asks her to give him a token of her purity that he may take into battle as he fights the forces of evil.

She insists vehemently that she is not Dulcinea but Aldonza. In a deeply moving song she tells of having been born in a ditch and of having been used and abused by hundreds of men. Again the Don refuses to see the reality of the situation and declares that he must have a token from the pure and beautiful Dulcinea.

The story continues in this vein, contrasting Don Quixote's holy madness with the brutal facts of the real world. At the end, the old man is

---

*Dale Wasserman and J. Darion, *Man of LaMancha* (New York: Random House, Inc.).

once again back in his bed at home, dying. Now he is in his right mind and no longer believes that he is a knight. And the most moving scene of the play is enacted when the people he has encountered come to his bedside and beg him not to change. For in a strange and miraculous way, each one has become a new person: the person whom Don Quixote saw in his pure and noble fantasy.

This is the power that you and I have if we love in the way that Jesus Christ has loved us. Our Lord calls us to a kind of "LaMancha madness." He wants us to go into the world and call forth goodness and truth, to affirm people and give them their true identity which may be deeply hidden.

The sociologist, the psychologist, and the educator look at life and describe it, but this does nothing to free people from the prisons of their past behavior. By contrast, we Christians, like our Lord, are called to a mission of affirmation.

When Jesus was here in the flesh, He called cowardly, unstable Simon a "rock" (Peter), long before there were any rocklike qualities evident. And Simon became Peter. The Old Testament tells the story of Jacob, whose name means "the cheat," or "supplanter," who wrestled with God by the brook Jabbok and arose with a new name: Israel, "the prince."

When Christians in large numbers discover this law of faith, life for human beings will be greatly changed.

Several years ago a series of extraordinary experiments was carried out by psychological researchers at Harvard. These experiments were designed to test the principle of the "self-fulfilling prophecy," or what we might call the power of faith. To begin, the researchers devised experiments using laboratory rats. They took rats which had precisely the same breeding and no particular laboratory conditioning, and divided them into two groups. One group of animals was given to researchers who were told that the rats were bred for "maze brightness"; the remaining group was given to other researchers who were advised that the animals could be expected to do poorly in maze training.

In one experiment after another, the expectations of the researchers were borne out in the performance of the animals. Those rats which were expected to learn quickly did, in fact, learn much more quickly than the others. There was no apparent reason for this aside from the expectation of the persons conducting the experiment.

The designers of the experiment were suitably impressed by these findings and by a wide variety of other tests involving both animals and human beings. They decided to see whether the "self-fulfilling prophecy" would work out in the setting of a public school as well as under the controlled conditions of a laboratory.

After making arrangements with the administrators of a school on the West Coast, the psychologists administered a standard test to all the students. They then informed the teachers that some of the students could be expected to "blossom" intellectually that year, while others could be expected not to show significant improvement. Actually, the two groups of students were chosen completely at random.

At the end of the school year, further tests revealed that those children who had been labeled "about to blossom" had done significantly better than the other students. What is more, the teachers reported more positive attitudes toward these students than toward others. Surprisingly, the teachers reacted *adversely* to progress among the students whom they did *not* expect to make unusual progress!

All of this is interesting in itself, but more than that it underscores the validity of the spiritual law that we have the power to elicit great things from those around us. We also have the power to inhibit others and to block their growth.

The lesson for Christians is very clear. When we meet a person in difficulty and see only a problem, we imprison that person in his or her problem. When by an act of faith we see the person as Jesus does, as unique, worthwhile, and with infinite possibilities, we begin to call forth a new being. Very simply, this is the power of affirmation.

Ugo Betti expresses this truth in his play, "The Burnt Flower Bed," which contains these lines:

> That's what's needed, don't you see: that. Nothing else matters half so much. To reassure one another. To answer each other. Perhaps only you can listen to me and not laugh. Everyone has inside himself—what shall I call it?—a piece of good news. Everyone is a very great, very important character. Every man must be persuaded, even if he is in rags, that he is immensely, immensely important. Everyone must respect him and make him respect himself, too. They must listen to him attentively. Don't stand on top of him. Don't stand in his light, but look at him with deference. Give him great, great hopes. He needs them, especially if he is young. Spoil him. Yes, make him grow proud.*

---

*From "The Burnt Flower Bed," by Ugo Betti, from *Three Plays*, translated by Henry Reed (New York: Grove Press, Inc.). Copyright © 1956 by Andreina Betti.

Ugo Betti is talking about affirmation and that is an essential quality in a Christian style. But there is a second dimension as well: personal vulnerability.

By nature and also by conditioning, our impulse is always to defend ourselves. Self-defense can take the form of belligerence, silence, ridicule, criticism, or proving that one is right. It all adds up to the same thing: invulnerability. Every natural force in us says, "Protect yourself. Don't let people get close to you. Don't let them know your weakness. Don't let them see where you are wrong."

Contrast this picture of natural man with the picture God shows us of Himself on the cross, when He made Himself naked and vulnerable in Jesus Christ.

Vulnerability poses a real problem for many Christians because we have made some false assumptions about what we are called to be and do. Too often we have been under the impression that in becoming Christians we have somehow become like God: that is, perfect, correct, proper, and beyond criticism. Such an attitude really misses the Christian style and is an obstacle in helping others.

The effective Christian is one who has discovered that God's love is most understandable and easily transmitted at this point of vulnerability. All of us are drawn to the person who is vulnerable in relationships with others—who demonstrates that he or she trusts us. Instinctively, we know that such a person is full of a new spirit—not a human spirit.

I once spent some time in a lay renewal center in England where a delightful Christian woman served as the lady warden. She seemed to love all the residents, and believe me, a lot of us were unlovely! Observing how she took time with each guest, I would conclude, "She really has found the victorious life. She's so naturally loving and saintly. Somehow she is made of different stuff from most of us." I found myself admiring that woman, but loving her from a distance and looking up to her. And by putting her on a pedestal, I somehow created a gulf between us.

Then one evening she was asked to make the evening address. She began by quoting her favorite bit of verse:

I wish I liked the human race,
I wish I liked its ugly face.
I wish when introduced to one
That I could say, "What jolly fun!"

Something inside me began to sing. Through her candid humor and her act of making herself vulnerable, I saw Christ in her in a new way. Then I realized that she is just like me, and the fantastic love she has for people is not innate, but it is the result of Christ's Spirit in her. What's more—I told myself—if it is Christ in her, then this kind of love is a possibility for me as well. To know that she found it as difficult as I do to love the unlovely spoke volumes about the power and love of Jesus Christ.

I have tried to put this principle to work in my own life. Sometimes, to be sure, there are no visible "results," and yet it is always worth the effort.

On a plane ride from Chicago to New York I was seated beside a man and his wife dressed in the official uniforms of Black Muslims. I had read enough about Black Muslims to have some conception of how these black people hated white people and Christians in particular.

For the first hour of the flight I made a few attempts to strike up a conversation with the couple, but without success. Finally, as I prayed silently, it seemed to me that God was saying something to me about being vulnerable. So at last I turned to the man beside me and asked if he would give me some advice.

He looked suspicious, but interested.

I mentioned that though I was a Christian I had great respect for Black Muslims, knowing them to be an extremely moral people, temperate, and with high ideals. Then I asked if they had difficulty communicating their dynamic faith to their teen-agers. As a Christian father, I said, I had problems in trying to communicate the Christian faith to my children.

Immediately, the man's defenses went down and he began to talk about the difficulty Black Muslims have in trying to lead and train their young people. We had a fascinating conversation during the last half of the plane ride, comparing notes on the similarity of the problems facing people of different religious persuasions.

This incident may seem trivial, and yet I believe that a rudimentary bridge was built and a relationship established, however tenuous, that enlarged the understanding of both myself and the Black Muslim. Christians need more and more to build bridges to the world of non-Christians by following their Lord's example of vulnerability. In this way we can begin to break down the barriers that make people strangers to one another. If we are both affirmative and vulnerable, the power of Christ in us can help us to share the great good news that we need no longer be strangers.

These principles are effective in the secular world as well. When I lived in New York City we witnessed a hotly contested mayoralty race, a three-way contest. The incumbent seemed certain to lose; the leading contender was almost a shoo-in as the race began. But when election day came, the incumbent managed to win a second term.

The following morning *The New York Times* ran a long article analyzing the election. In the opinion of those reporters who had followed the campaign closely, the turning point came because the incumbent, who seemed to have no real chance of victory, was able to ask for help even from his political enemies, while the front-runner, who seemed assured of victory, was unable to ask for help even from his friends.

This to me was a striking example of personal vulnerability in public life. It reinforced my conviction that Christians ought to seek this quality earnestly.

Max Beerbohm once said that all the world is divided into two classes of people: the guests and the hosts. We all know that a guest is someone who is invulnerable, who is waited upon and showered with attention. A host, on the other hand, is one who puts his guests at ease and affirms their worth in a thousand different ways and makes himself vulnerable to them, giving up his privacy and providing food and lodging.

It seems to me that Jesus Christ, who is "the Host" in all of life, is calling those who believe in Him to become hosts in every situation; to become those who can be vulnerable, put other people at ease, love them, listen to them, and affirm them.

You and God

The direct connection between our relationship with God and our relationship with others is affirmed and reaffirmed countless times in Scripture. John said, "How can you love God, whom you have not seen, if you cannot love your brother whom you have seen?"

To love is to trust, and to trust is to reveal those things about yourself that could give someone else the weapons with which to hurt you. Until we can be this vulnerable we cannot truly love. And it is not enough to be vulnerable to God; we must also be vulnerable to others.

4

You and God

Whoever you are, wherever you live, whatever your values or philosophy of life, you can't escape the necessity of living in four relationships.

Each person must relate in some way to God (by whatever name He is called); to himself; to the significant others in his life (those with whom he lives and works intimately); and to the world (everyone outside his immediate sphere, whether down the street or halfway around the globe). The quality of these relationships determines whether one truly *lives* or merely muddles through life. The good news of the gospel is that Jesus Christ can enter into a human life and redeem it in all four of these dimensions or relationships.

The most basic and important relationship is the one which exists between a human being and God. I am convinced that it is impossible to escape this relationship even if one denies the very existence of a Supreme Being. The people I have known who professed not to believe in God have spent a great deal of time denying Him, fighting Him, burying Him, explaining Him away, or attempting to prove others wrong who do believe in Him—and this constitutes a relationship. Perhaps there are those who are totally indifferent to God, who never give Him a second thought, but I have never met such an individual.

Built into every human being there seems to be some instinctive sense that there is Someone or Something "out there" that cannot be ignored.

To some, God is the great unknown; to others, a tyrannical monster; to still others, a quixotic puppeteer who manipulates the universe by pulling strings at random. Our conceptions of God are determined by our training and experiences. Actually, there is a tremendous number of diverse influences that play a part in formulating our ideas about God.

Merely accepting Christian doctrine does not mean that one will enter immediately into a right relationship with God. One can be doctrinally sound and relationally handicapped, crippled, or impotent. It is quite possible to know all the classic Christian teachings about the nature of God and His dealings with mankind and still treat Him as though He were irrelevant or far removed from real life.

A right relationship begins with believing the good news that God proclaims in Jesus Christ: "I love you. I love you as you are. I love you unconditionally. I have already given myself to you totally, and now all I ask is that you begin to respond to my love and my commitment to you by committing to me all of yourself that you are able to give."

God's love does not depend on any virtue in us or on our achievements. But the nature of His love is such that He does not leave us as He finds us. When someone begins the adventure of faith, God says to him, in effect: "I am going to begin to change you. Programmed into your inner computer, through glands and genes and circumstances and experiences, is an inability to love totally. I love you so much that I want to change all of those intricate wires of experience, sense, and thought that make you an unknowable, unrelatable person. It may take a thousand years of reprogramming to make you a lover of people, of me, and of yourself, but I promise that I will continue relentlessly until you have been totally transformed. I'll begin at the moment you give me your life, and I will not stop until all your quirks and defense mechanisms and subterfuges and alibis are gone and you are a transparent, relatable person."

This is what I hear God saying in the gospel.

And more: "But even after a thousand years of this process of change, I will not love you one bit more than I love you now, at the moment of your commitment to me; or one bit more than I loved you at the moment of your conception or your birth. My love for you is total and unconditional. I am not trying to change you so that I can love you. I love you, and because I do, I want to change you."

If this is what the cross is all about, if this is what Jesus Christ has accomplished by His Incarnation and Atonement, then we are talking about good news that is too good to be true.

News "too good to be true" is always difficult to cope with. A vacation-time incident one summer provided me with a vivid illustration of this. We were spending our holiday by a beautiful lake in Canada—my wife and I, our three children, and one of our daughter's friends. Every morning the two boys and I would go out on the lake before breakfast and try to catch a couple of fish.

One evening my daughter and her friend said, "Why can't we go fishing tomorrow morning instead of the boys?"

"Great," I said.

The next morning found the two girls and me out on the lake in our flat-bottom boat with its antique outboard motor. Our luck was not good. Heading back toward shore, I was sitting in the middle of the boat untangling a line. Christine was steering and her friend Jean was sitting in the front. "Gee, Mister Larson," Jean said, "I'm sorry we didn't catch a big one to impress the boys with."

No sooner were these words out of her mouth than a fifteen-inch Northern Pike jumped out of the lake, hit me on the side of the face, and fell into the boat, where it flip-flopped wildly at my feet.

As you read this, do you believe it? I've told this story to a great many people and the skeptics invariably outnumber the believers.

That, of course, was our problem: how to make this good news believable. As we pulled in to the dock, the boys were waiting for us. I held up the fish and one of the boys said, "Not bad. How did you catch him?"

You may be sure that we spent most of the morning trying to convince the boys that the fish really had jumped into the boat. As a matter of fact, I'm not sure they ever were convinced.

This is the problem Christians have when they try to express the love of God in Jesus Christ to someone who has never experienced it. You walk up to some unsuspecting person and begin to talk about God. You tell him that God loves him just as he is, unconditionally, no strings attached; that all God wants is to have him respond to that love with his own love and commitment.

That person can't even hear you. No one has ever demonstrated such love to him. The good news of God's love for us is simply too good to be true.

Our inability to hear this good news causes us to misinterpret various New Testament admonitions. For example, we hear the verse, "Be ye perfect, even as your heavenly father is perfect," and somehow this comes to mean that if we will be pure or without fault or moral blemish or theological confusion, God will love us. In point of fact, "be perfect" in the original language of the New Testament really implies that God wants me to become the perfect me. It doesn't mean that I am to be like God. It means for me to stand so firmly and securely in the love of God that I can dare to be myself and no one else.

This, to me, is one of the great marks of a right relationship to God. It means that I can begin to talk to God as the man that I am at the moment and not as the man I would like to be or as the man that I think God would like me to be. It means that I begin to believe the incredible love of God, and thus honor Him by affirming that love through my own openness and trust and honesty.

A friend of mine taught me a great lesson one morning as we were having a cup of coffee together and getting ready to face the tasks of the day. We were in the habit of "checking in" with each other as often as possible, to listen to each other and to share whatever concerns were on our minds. That particular morning when I asked my friend how he was doing, he said, "Terrible. I had a fight with my wife last night and we went to bed not speaking to each other, sleeping back to back. But this morning she gave me a kiss and said, 'Honey, I love you.' "

"What did you say?" I asked eagerly.

"I said, 'Well, I don't love you and I don't love myself and I don't love God. I can't think of anybody that I do love. But I'll tell you this: I'm going to pray this morning and I believe that sometime in the near future God will straighten me out because He loves me. He will make me able to love again. And when He does, I promise to put you first on the list!' "

This kind of honesty frees us of the need to pretend and allows us to be ourselves before God and before people. It affirms our trust in a God who will not only forgive but will also change us into the kinds of people He would like us to be and that we ourselves would like to be.

Isn't this the dynamic behind David, the Old Testament king and psalmist? David was a man whom God called "a man after my own heart." But he was not a good man, and if he were alive today I doubt that he could get the endorsement of a pulpit nominating committee or the credentials to enter a theological seminary. Among other things, David was a thief, an adulterer, and a murderer. Nevertheless, he was a man after God's own heart. To understand this is to plumb the depths of God's love for humanity.

When David saw his sins, he admitted them before God and man and made no defense for himself. But he went beyond mere confession. He believed he was forgiven even though he was a sinner.

There is a marvelous scene in the Bible describing David's behavior when he had rediscovered again the amazing grace of God. He danced before the Ark in the sight of all the people of Israel. His wife Michal shouted at him, "Come in; you're making a fool of yourself." Not only was David dancing, but he was wearing some sort of kilt or short skirt and apparently he had no jockey shorts on. Michal, the daughter of a king, was outraged and humiliated.

"I can't stop!" David shouted back, continuing to dance wildly before the Ark, celebrating the good news that God forgives and justifies sinners. Having confessed openly his own unrighteousness, David was free to celebrate the grace of God.

Keith Miller has a great insight in his book, *The Taste of New Wine*,* where he talks about the dynamics of confession. He suggests that when you have confessed your sin to God, you must then admit your faults before man. He suggests that when you have let somebody else know what God has revealed to you about your sins, you will never again waste time pretending that you are righteous.

How many of us confuse the good news of God with "religion" and have wasted our time and destroyed ourselves and others by having to maintain some kind of righteous stance? The gospel is for those who understand that they are not righteous, and who can claim the gift that God offers: His forgiveness and cleansing and unconditional love.

The direct connection between our relationship with God and our relationship with others is affirmed and reaffirmed countless times in Scripture. John said, "How can you love God, whom you have not seen, if you cannot love your brother whom you have seen?"

To love is to trust, and to trust is to reveal those things about yourself that could give someone else the weapons with which to hurt you. Until we can be this vulnerable we cannot truly love. And it is not enough to be vulnerable to God; we must also be vulnerable to our brothers.

One of the greatest Christians I know has been for many years the head of the world's largest conservative faith mission. Norman is an Englishman and one of God's unique and delightful saints. He tells about the time, years after his conversion, when he was in East Africa with the Christians in Uganda during their great revival. In their vulnerable style

---

*Keith Miller, *The Taste of New Wine* (Waco, Texas: Word Books, 1965).

of life he saw a contrast to his own pretensions. One night after being with these Christians who believe in "walking in the light," as the phrase from John's first epistle has it, Norman went back to his hut and got on his knees and began to confess to God his sins against his wife, who was still in England. He began to confess his shortness of temper and his irritability.

In the midst of this confession to God, he suddenly heard the still, small voice say, "Norman, don't tell me. *I told you.* Go and tell your wife."

This is why confession must be not only from man to God but from man to man. It is God Himself who reveals where we are missing the mark. To tell Him about our sins is simply to acknowledge that we have heard what He has been telling us. The real test comes when we can let go of our righteousness and tell at least one other human being about this new insight that God has given us regarding our disobedience or unfaithfulness.

We speak about the Christian style as one of both vulnerability and affirmation. In our relationship to God we realize that the good news is not our response to a doctrine or a theology, but a response to a person. The gospel is embodied in a person affirming us: Jesus Christ saying, "I love you unconditionally. Will you give me your life?"

We cannot respond to this with "true" or "false" any more than we can respond to the statement, "I love you. Will you marry me?" by saying "true" or "false." We can only say "yes" or "no." To say yes is to return affirmation with affirmation. We affirm God by yielding to Him, even as He has affirmed us by giving us Himself in the person of Jesus Christ.

A true, affirmative commitment to Jesus Christ may be as simple and prosaic as this: "Well, Lord, I love you, and here is my life. I've changed what I can, but there are certain things I can't change. I have certain assets and liabilities that are a part of my birthright and training. I've got some sins of my own making. Some of them I'm stuck with. And Lord, I can't promise that I'll be good. I want to be good, but I can't promise that I will be. But here I am. I give myself to you. Do with me what you will."

Sometimes people find it hard to hear the gospel in its essence because they are so preoccupied with the laws, rules, and commandments found in the Bible. Standards of ethics and moral laws are not to be confused with the gospel.

It reminds me of a time when my wife, fed up with the condition in which our children left the bathroom, made the following sign and hung it on the inside of the bathroom door: "Do not leave the bathroom until you have cleaned out the washbowl, hung up the towels, put the soap away, and picked up your clothes."

I can't remember that these rules made much of an impact on the behavior of the children, but I do know that some of our guests would come out of the bathroom sheepishly reporting that they had observed all the rules.

This can be a parable of how God has dealt with us. He has given us rules to let us know where we have failed and how we might live if life is to be abundant. But we are not Christians because we keep the rules. The rules point out where we have failed and remind us of the need to respond to God's offer of forgiveness and love and a new spirit.

When we enter into a right relationship with God, just how much change or improvement can we expect? In one sense we never change. The new creation that God has promised us if we accept Jesus Christ begins as He starts to deal with some of our inner conditions that do not change. For example, if we are full of guilt, it can help us to discover grace. If we are full of fear and give it to God, our very fear becomes faith. Our loneliness, transformed by God, can help us to love. Critical-ness can become discernment. Phoniness or hypocrisy, when confessed to God and man, can become freedom.

Grace, faith, love, discernment, and freedom are all, therefore, the "products" of inner conditions given to God—but the inner conditions do not disappear. We have a choice of living with these inner conditions, unacknowledged, unsurrendered, and uncommitted to God. Or we can give all these qualities into God's keeping and see them transformed.

It is much like the case of an alcoholic who joins AA. He never ceases to be an alcoholic, but by the power of God he can live free of alcohol and he can become a part of God's creative purpose in setting other alcoholics free. Nevertheless, all the while he is a part of this process, discovering sobriety and sharing his newfound strength with others, he reminds himself publicly and privately that he is still an alcoholic. This crucial point in the AA program has made it unpalatable to some doctors and psychologists and also to some alcoholics who have managed to find sobriety in other ways; yet I believe it to be realistic and in large part responsible for the success of AA in helping those caught in alcoholism.

Again we are reminded of King David. A sinner and a rebel, he could nonetheless face his faults and stand in God's presence, celebrating the good news that he was loved, forgiven, cleansed, and capable of transformation. He is a model for all of us.

The Old Testament provides us with another character study that gives the other side of the coin. In the ancient poetic drama of Job, we find revealed the tragic example of a good man who missed this central message of God's grace.

Job *is* a good man—far better than David. With all his problems and plagues, the death of his children and the loss of his property, and finally the terrible illness that besets him, Job is able to keep trusting God. But when his so-called comforters try to find the flaw in Job's nature that made God punish him so cruelly, Job defends himself and declares that there is nothing in his nature deserving of punishment.

Job's self-defense was his problem. He was a good man who missed the point; King David was a bad man who did not have to justify God or defend himself.

Perhaps this is the radical nature of the Christian style which we should learn to demonstrate for the world. The Christian is not always right, always virtuous, or always guided. Not at all. He is often wrong, errs frequently, and makes many wrong turns. But he is someone who does not have to defend or justify himself—he has been freed by the grace of God from the need to be someone or something other than himself.

Martin Luther said that a Christian ought to love God and sin boldly. Does this sound shocking? It should not, for Luther believed that all human endeavors and activities are tinged with sin: that man is incapable of complete unselfishness. However, there is another sense in which we might take Luther's advice. To me it means that the Christian, wherever he lives or in whatever century, ought to be adventuring and trying new things, totally unafraid of failure. We live in a world where failure is always at hand, and where guilt is bound to rise up at every turn to plague us.

Take, for example, the case of a man who has been working late night after night for a long time. One evening he says to his wife, "Tomorrow, dear, I will be home early. We're going out to the best restaurant in town to celebrate."

But the next day as he is about to leave his place of work, a man for whom he has been concerned comes in to say, "I need you right now. I am in desperate trouble."

Our friend is then faced with a choice of whether to fail his wife and stay with the man in need, or fail the man and go home to a promised date with his wife. Whatever he chooses to do, he cannot be sure that it is right. Guidance may not come instantly.

The mark of an authentic Christian is that if he decides to stay and help his colleague, when he goes home hours later to a furious wife, he does not justify himself. Rather, he says, "Honey, I prayed, and I did what I thought was right. But perhaps I was wrong. Please forgive me."

It seems to me impossible for a Christian to live so cautiously and circumspectly that he never gets into a situation like this. When one is totally and vulnerably involved in the needs of people, conflicts are bound to arise and there are resentments and hurt feelings. The person who tries desperately to avoid conflict, to avoid sin, is acting out his or her conviction that God cannot or will not forgive, that God's grace is not sufficient.

The new person in Christ, like King David, can move out into creative relationships and adventure, in spite of the risk of failure. When failure happens, he or she does not justify that failure by blaming God's guidance.

It is a matter of desperate importance that Christians understand the unavoidability of guilt. We are not people who because we are Christians cease to be guilty; we are not always guided or spirit-filled. Rather, we are those who no longer have to pretend that we are the innocent party in dozens of relationships and situations day by day.

There was a real turning-point in my life when I came to a new understanding of the nature and meaning of public worship. I belong to a denomination that holds communion to be tremendously holy and sacred, and for this reason in our tradition we have communion four times a year, or at most once a month. It is always an occasion of great solemnity, with special effects accompanying it, both by the choir and by the elders who serve.

Therefore, I have been bothered for years by the matter-of-factness with which Roman Catholics and Episcopalians seem to regard communion. The Sacrament is administered every Sunday, and communicants come forward to receive it as casually as if they were coming forward to accept a cup of tea. At least this is how it appeared to me.

Then one Sunday I was worshiping in the Episcopal church in my home town, and when the invitation was given to come forward for communion, the theology behind this tradition, which provides the Sacrament often and in a matter-of-fact way, suddenly made sense to me.

Here were people who had inherited a centuries-old tradition—a tradition which makes provision for the fact that we are rebellious, sinful creatures who generate enough guilt every week to destroy us. What can we do with this kind of guilt? We cannot sing it away, or study it away, or erase it with good works, or even pray it away. There is only one means possible by which we can deal with sin and rebellion in life: we can confess it and receive the grace of God which is sacramentally remembered in the elements of bread and wine.

This matter-of-factness represented a much more profound understanding of the nature of man and the nature of God and the celebration of good news than did my own tradition, which makes the occasion so special and so solemn.

Without accepting God's love and forgiveness day by day and week by week, we will surely be swamped by the bilgewater that seeps through the leaky hulls of our lives. At least once a week we can honestly face ourselves and honestly deal with God's offer to forgive and cleanse. This is the source of the Christian's joy and celebration. It is not that we are no longer guilty, but that we have accepted God's answer for our guilt and gladly celebrate and bear witness to it.

Much of the literature of our time provides insights into the nature of guilt. For example, Arthur Miller's play, "After the Fall,"* deals in a moving and provocative way with one man's experience of guilt. Those who read this play and audiences who see it can hardly escape the conclusion that in the hero, Quentin, Arthur Miller is presenting a thinly veiled account of his own life.

Quentin talks about himself and his experiences. He tells about his first marriage, the incessant fights with his wife, the need to justify everything he did. Like many of us, he is touchy and defensive.

Then one day he asks himself why in these hundreds of situations of no real consequence he finds it necessary always to defend himself and be absolved. He says that he has lived his life as if there were a judge sitting on a high bench, watching everything he did and judging his failures. At last he looks up and realizes that the bench is empty. He no longer has to justify himself, for there is no one to judge him.

Did this insight, expressed through the character Quentin, make a difference in Arthur Miller's own life? A colleague of mine became acquainted with someone who had worked closely with Miller in the preparation of a later play. This man expressed great admiration for the playwright and described him as someone who could take criticism calmly, accept suggestions, and rework the script over and over again through countless revisions—all without a show of temper and without

*Arthur Miller, *After the Fall* (New York: The Viking Press, Inc.).

the kind of self-justification for which writers and artists are notorious. Apparently, the transformation had been made.

As a Christian, I cannot agree with Arthur Miller that there is "no one on the bench." But in his freedom, he is way ahead of most of us.

We can look at the bench and see it occupied by the Lord of creation and the Savior of the world, Jesus Christ Himself. He is the judge who has come to take our place and deal with our sins. Therefore, we can be free to live life in a different way—not because the bench is empty but because the judge has declared us innocent. He has told us that He loves us. He has affirmed us. He has been vulnerable. And we can celebrate news "too good to be true" by being vulnerable before Him and before our brothers and sisters.

Truly, we are no longer strangers.

You and Your Inner Self

The gospel is good news for a universal race of those who don't fit in: losers, odd ones, the peculiar, and the out of step—"not the righteous, but sinners."
It is just such people that God loved when He came into the world in Jesus Christ "to seek and to save that which was lost." In Him we are no longer strangers—to God, to one another, or even to ourselves.

5

You and Your Inner Self

"Who am I?" is one of the great, persistent questions of our era. It is characteristic of contemporary life that vast numbers of people feel alienated not only from their world but also from themselves. With the constantly changing patterns of society and the crumbling of familiar structures, more and more individuals tend to feel "out of touch." They ask themselves, "Who am I? Where do I belong?" and are frightened by the answers that confront them.

Everyone has a relationship with himself, good or bad. The gospel is good news in this area, too, for it can mean the end of loneliness, alienation, and separation. For me, the impact of the gospel in this realm—my relationship with myself—has provided an exciting breakthrough. For too many years I was afraid to look at myself realistically or to examine the person inside me. I could not classify myself with those who basically like themselves; I was among the vast throng who fear that if they really knew what they were like inside, they would be unable to face the mirror without despising what they saw reflected there.

When Jesus Christ comes to us and affirms us through His own vulnerability, He asks us to become vulnerable—but also to begin affirming ourselves. He asks us to affirm ourselves not because we are perfect but because He loves and affirms us. And in the great words of Scripture, "If God be for us, who can be against us?"

The need for self-affirmation is by no means confined to those who have obvious lacks: physical, emotional, mental, or social. Even those who appear to "have everything"—to "have it made" in the world's eyes—may be sadly lacking in self-appreciation.

I once had a long talk with a lovely New York debutante, someone who at first glance appeared to be in a truly enviable position. We spoke about Jesus Christ and how much He loves each one of us. Then we talked about who this young woman was in her inner life. At last we finished our conversation with some prayer, believing that Christ affirmed her and that she could affirm herself, not because she was everything she ought to be but because God loved her as she was.

A few days later I received a letter from this young woman, which she has given me permission to quote in part: "Your honesty meant so much. . . . Although this [love and acceptance] is a vital part of the Christian group to which I belong, I had never experienced it in the way I did with you.

"The most amazing thing happened last Thursday night in the middle of our small group meeting. I suddenly realized that I am a person—a real person. . . . This realization that I don't have to depend on other people for approval, or to get ideas from them as I constantly did, was so staggering that it was only through sheer restraint that I didn't jump right out of my chair. How wonderful to be able to be myself!

"I really was a mess when I came in to see you. The more I think about what I said—or didn't say—it seems pitiful . . . but I'm afraid the real me is what came out. It doesn't matter now, though, because I am so completely changed. Introspection once seemed an important part of my Christian life but it no longer seems necessary. Now that Jesus has all of me, the bad along with the good, He can take the bad and use it the way He wants to with no objections from me."

Then she went on to describe how relationships were changing in her daily life: one with a friend, one with her mother, and one with a colleague at work. The latter had changed in such a way that she had a new attitude not only toward her co-workers but also to the job itself.

Jesus must have had this in mind when He said, "If the son shall make you free, you shall be free indeed." Free not only to love God, but to love ourselves.

Loving ourselves ought to be easy because we are usually so preoccupied with ourselves. But the two things can be quite different. In my own life I have discovered that preoccupation with myself can be a very misleading guide.

One morning while riding the train to work I was talking with a colleague. He and I frequently acted as priests to each other in terms of listening, counsel, and prayer. That morning I was telling him about a dreadful thing I had done the day before in minimizing and humiliating a Christian friend.

. This third person had done something that seemed to me way out of line, but the way in which I reprimanded him was even more so. Now I was suffering pangs of guilt over my behavior, like many times in the past when I had lost my temper and had to ask forgiveness and make restitution.

At any rate, I was telling my colleague about the terrible thing I had done, and how little sleep I'd had because of my troubled conscience. After I had gone on at some length about my own unworthiness and unfaithfulness, my friend said, "Bruce, what kind of advice would you give to me if I were in your shoes right now?"

I thought about it for a minute and then replied, "I'd say, 'What else is new? Claim the forgiveness that God has for you in Christ; accept yourself as you are; don't be surprised that you failed. And then ask your friend to forgive you. Make restitution as best you can.' "

"Why don't you do that?"

I acknowledged that my own advice was pretty good, and then my friend continued, "I'll tell you why you don't do it. It's because you're basically conceited. If one of your friends failed in the way you did, you would be most understanding and accepting and permissive. But you are harder on yourself than on others because you think you are better than we are. You think you shouldn't sin the way we sin."

I knew that my brother was speaking the truth, and for a moment I hated him. But after a bit I could thank him for being God's instrument in revealing to me an unpleasant truth about myself.

You see, for years I had called my breast-beating, "humility," when all the time it was really conceit.

It has made a tremendous difference in my life to realize that I can affirm myself if I really believe in the cross and can be vulnerable before God and accept His tremendous affirmation of me in Jesus Christ. If I am really what I claim to be, a sinner in the eyes of God, then I shouldn't be surprised when I fail. At the very moment of failure, I should be able to pray, "Well, Lord, I shouldn't expect much more. As a matter of fact, I'm surprised that I behave so well so much of the time.

But now I thank you for pointing out that I have failed, and for the conscience that stabs me. I claim your forgiveness, I accept your love, and I will ask my brother to forgive me as I make restitution."

The key is not in covering up our badness, but in facing it quite honestly. The moment we face it we can believe that Jesus Christ is saying, "I love you now just as much as I loved you when you were performing admirably a few hours or a few days ago."

Jesus understood our need for self-love. He commanded us to love our neighbor as ourselves. One cannot love his neighbor until he loves himself, so it is tremendously important that we accept the love of God for us in our badness as well as in our goodness.

The psychological implications of healthy self-love are obvious. But until quite recently I had not realized that there are social implications as well. The importance of this aspect of the problem was first brought to my attention by a city planner in a Midwestern metropolis.

A number of Christian leaders had gathered in that city to meet with community leaders in preparation for an ecumenical city-wide mission. Our aim was to offer the combined services of several Christian groups to the city if they would have us.

It was rather difficult trying to describe to the community leaders just what we represented and hoped to offer, and in an attempt to make our position clear we talked about the four "basic relationships" of which this book speaks.

When we had completed our presentation, one of the city planners rose to his feet and said something like this, "Listen, I know about the cities of America. This has been my life. And I want to say that I am convinced that what is killing our cities is the acid of self-hate in their bloodstreams. If you have some way to get rid of this acid of self-hate, you have the answer to what is plaguing America's cities today."

When pressed for a further explanation, the city official expressed the opinion that self-hate is what makes people misuse and destroy property, other people, and even themselves.

If he is right, and I am inclined to think he is, then we have pin-pointed another area in which the gospel can speak relevantly: the area of self-love and self-acceptance. People who can look fully into the amazing love of God as we see it in Jesus Christ, and can love themselves because of this love, can begin to provide healthy solutions to many of our perplexing social problems.

Self-love is not an easy thing. As a matter of fact, it takes the power of God to make it a reality.

I realized this anew during a week-long retreat for seminary seniors. During one of our sessions with the students we asked them to jot down five words to represent five things that were liabilities or sins in their lives, and to raise their hands as soon as they had completed their lists. In fifteen seconds several hands went up. In three-quarters of a minute nearly every student had raised his hand.

Then we asked them to turn over their pieces of paper and to compile a list of five things that were good about them. "Write down five assets or strengths that God has built into you that make you unique. Try to use a single word to describe each asset. Start writing," we urged, again asking that the students raise their hands when their lists were finished. After forty-five seconds, one student raised his hand. In a minute and a half, no more than ten percent of the young men had completed their lists. In fact, some students were *never* able to think of five good things about themselves! It was clear that somehow our Christian training had made us focus on our sins and not on our assets.

We have tried this experiment in a variety of situations, with men and women of all ages, and the results are quite similar. Nearly everyone has difficulty assessing his own strengths; hardly anyone has trouble naming his liabilities.

But certainly we have as many assets as liabilities; as many strengths as sins! For some reason, however, we have concentrated on the negative aspects of life until we are unable to thank God for the gifts He has lavished on every one of us.

This is, I believe, part of the alienation that makes us strangers to ourselves. The gospel is good news because it enables us to begin honestly to admit our failures, and also honestly to admit our strengths. We can begin to see ourselves as we really are.

Once I heard Richard Halverson, chaplain of the United States Senate, give an unforgettable talk on the subject of glory. It gave me a new insight into the nature of glory, and some idea of why the Gospels speak so much about the glory that is to be revealed through Jesus Christ. Dick Halverson pointed out that nature is glorious when it is simply "being itself": the sun giving forth heat and light; a flower blooming and emitting its own fragrance. Our glory as human beings is likewise simply to be ourselves, with all of our assets and liabilities.

Perhaps many of us who have been Christians for years have missed the full impact of the gospel if we have not discovered what it is to be ourselves: loved by God, irreplaceable in His sight, unique among our fellowmen. Somehow we have been conditioned to maximize our sins and minimize our strengths.

One of my particular failures is that so often I have tried to be like Jesus. Keith Miller has shed light on the fallacy of this position by pointing out that we only imitate someone when he is absent. If we are impressed by someone, then consciously or unconsciously we try to copy him when he is away. But to copy someone when he is present is ridiculous because the original is there. To try to be like Jesus is to say to the world, in a way, that He is absent and that we must take His place.

A Christian is most truly a Christian when he is most truly himself. At this point he can bear witness to the fact that there stands one in our midst who is the Lord and Savior, the Creator and Redeemer of life. He is with us, and He needs no one to substitute for Him.

The first time I had the privilege of spending time with Dr. Paul Tournier was during a five-day workshop in Spain for doctors, clergy and lay leaders. It was a rare opportunity to meet the Christian writer and psychiatrist whose influence has been so widespread.

One of the doctors asked Paul Tournier if it is possible to be a phony Christian. When the question was translated by our interpreter from English into French, Dr. Tournier replied immediately with a whimsical smile, "Mais, oui. C'est moi" ("Of course. It's me").

He then went on to explain that he is often caught in the trap of trying to be something he is not—trying to measure up to the image people have of him, of living up to his reputation, of trying to solve his patients' problems instead of allowing God to solve them.

With a great deal of honesty and charm he talked about the Paul Tournier who is so much like each one of us. The more he acknowledged his own phoniness and how unreal he can be at times, the more Jesus Christ was revealed through the life of this man. If he had answered the question with guarded reserve, speaking in general terms about the perils of phoniness, the effect would have been entirely different. By skirting the issue he would have implied that he was Christlike and never phoney. But this would have minimized the witness that Christ could make to us through a man who dared to be himself—and who assumed that Jesus Christ would be Himself when Paul Tournier was being himself.

Our fear of being ourselves is very likely one of the things that makes us ill, physically and mentally as well as spiritually. For example, there is an interesting theory on why women usually outlive men. The theory is that men have a mental picture of what they should be in the eyes of the world; they feel that they are supposed to keep their emotions and fears bottled up inside, and therefore become, in the words of Sidney Jourard of the University of Florida, "men whom nobody knows."

Dr. Jourard says that there is no evidence to show that female tissue is intrinsically more durable than male tissue. It is his opinion that the probable reason for the longer life of women can be found in their method of relating to the world.* Men think they should appear objective and tough, striving, achieving and unsentimental. And above all, unexpressive of the person inside. They are never, of course, to show weakness, and if a man shows his feelings he is afraid that he will be regarded as inferior to his fellows. Therefore he is obliged to hide much of his real self.

We know that when we are forced to hide who we are and what we feel, we are under terrific stress. This can cause extreme fatigue and even the breakdown of body tissues and the malfunction of vital organs. It is stress that shortens life—stress which cannot be acknowledged and dealt with adequately.

Women are usually much more willing to reveal who they are and to disclose facts about themselves, to open up and talk about things that a man simply will not discuss. According to this theory, the shortened life span of many men can be accounted for by the fact that they are constantly striving to be something they are not.

Obviously this theory cannot apply in all cases, but it is interesting and I think valid in a tremendous number of situations. When a man's self is hidden from everybody, it is also usually hidden from himself. This encourages illness, mental breakdown, and premature death. Surely this is one of the reasons Jesus Christ told us to love ourselves and to tell ourselves the truth about who we are and how we feel. To be honest with one's self and with others is truly a healthful way to live.

All of us, even those of us who know the love of God, tend to become liars when we are left to our own devices. Perhaps this is why Jesus said that where two or three are gathered together in His name, He will be in the midst of them. This is what the Body of Christ is all about. We need one another so that we can have some measure of objectivity—and even prophetic insight—as we begin to explore our inner self.

Psychologists have devoted a great deal of time and effort to discover the defense mechanisms people use: mechanisms which allow us to lie to ourselves. Hundreds, perhaps thousands of such mechanisms are known, and not one of us left to ourselves is completely free of the traps that

---

*Sidney Jourard, *The Transparent Self* (Princeton, N.J.: D. Van Nostrand Co., Inc.).

lead to spiritual, mental, and physical illness. But if we can open up to one another, there is hope that God can speak through someone else the words of truth we need to hear.

Some time ago I came to know a clergyman who had suffered intermittently for many years from a personal problem. During World War II he had been discharged from the army because of emotional difficulties. Ever since, this pastor had carried around a load of guilt. What plagued him was the thought that he had deceived the medical board in order to obtain a discharge. So conscience-stricken was he that he had even written to the Secretary of the Army offering to reenlist to fulfill the term of service that he had avoided.

For many hours over a period of several days I talked with this sensitive brother pastor about his problem. I realized that he knew about the love of God and His forgiveness in Jesus Christ. When I asked what advice he would give to someone else who came to him with this problem, he gave all the right answers about accepting the possible guilt and claiming Christ's love and forgiveness. But even though he knew the right answers, his problem persisted.

At last we invited the pastor's wife to join us, and the three of us talked over the situation. Something she said provided the clue to the real problem. What this man really feared was not the thought that he had fooled the army medical examiners about his emotional state. His family had a history of mental illness, and what he feared was that the medical examiners were perfectly correct and that he *was* emotionally unstable. It was this that he could not face. And because he could not face this, he chose to struggle with an unreal problem that was less threatening to his psychic stability.

When the three of us faced the real problem, one could sense the miracle of God revealing a man to himself as he was. The pastor had become lonely, separated from people, and ineffective in his ministry, all because he could not face the truth. When he was able to do so, and when God's love and forgiveness were accepted, something new and dynamic began. The new creation promised in Jesus Christ began to appear.

This illustrates what remarkable things can happen when we are in the company of others who can help us to think through hidden fears and to begin to experience God's love and acceptance. It is vitally important to each of us to have a good relationship with himself. In such a relationship, we can discover the truth about ourselves and acknowledge it in the presence of another, and as a result, we can believe that we are loved and affirmed by God in this truth.

Because of God's tremendous love and acceptance in Christ, we need no longer be strangers to ourselves, but can accept ourselves and even delight in being the peculiar creatures that we are. The gospel is good news not only because of God's unconditional love, but because each of us can join the human race as an odd, unique sort of being.

A few years ago I saw a marvelous piece of communication on a subway wall in New York City. The subway walls are irresistible attractions to graffiti artists of all ages—people who draw pictures and scrawl messages: some of them obscene, some sad, and some funny. A certain advertising poster showed a very austere, proper, older gentleman recommending a product, and someone—perhaps a little boy writing the dirtiest thing he could think of—had sketched a balloon coming out of the man's mouth containing the words, "I like grils,"

Underneath, someone had written with a felt-tipped pen, "It's girls, stupid, not grils."

And below that, in still another handwriting style, someone else had added, "But what about us grils?"

Herein is the marvelous good news of the gospel: when we are honest with ourselves and with a few others, we find that all of us are really "grils"—oddballs and misfits. The gospel is good news for a universal race of those who don't fit in: losers, odd ones, the peculiar, and the out of step—"not the righteous, but sinners."

It is just such people that God loved when He came into the world in Jesus Christ "to seek and to save that which was lost." In Him we are no longer strangers—to God, to one another, or even to ourselves.

You and Your
    "Significant Others"

*Samuel Johnson once wrote, "Marriage has many
pains, but celibacy has no pleasures." I'd like to
paraphrase this for the Christian, married or single:
"This radical style of life in Christ has many
pains, but anything less has few pleasures."
The more we guard our lives and the more we
protect ourselves, the more lonely and withdrawn
we become. As we discover in Jesus Christ both the
example we need and the power to live as He lived,
we go through the pain into a life of deep, loving
relationships. Through this kind of radical
obedience we discover that we are no longer
strangers.*

6

You and Your
"Significant Others"

No one needs to be convinced that loneliness is one of the great tragic themes of contemporary life. So many novelists, poets, playwrights, and filmmakers have dealt with this theme that one wonders if the pulpit has anything new to add about sin in this area. Perhaps, therefore, we need to speak about the *good news* in terms of meaningful relationships between "significant people"—those with whom we live and work and play on a day-by-day basis—made possible through the grace of God.

In his plays, Tennessee Williams dealt again and again with the problem of loneliness and alienation. He seems to speak for a whole generation of literary prophets. In one of his earlier plays, Williams wrote, "If loneliness is as prevalent as we are led to believe that it is, then surely the great sin of our time must be to be lonely alone."

Apparently there is nothing contemporary man wants more than to be rescued from estrangement with his fellowmen. It is precisely at this point that God's great promise to us in Christ, that we are no longer strangers, touches modern man most poignantly and relevantly.

We have said that the Christian style of life, made possible by God's love for us in Jesus Christ, enables us to become vulnerable, to affirm ourselves and to affirm others. How difficult this is without Christ! The walls of separation grow up between parents and children, husbands and wives, friends and colleagues, simply because we cannot say the affirmative thing about someone else and because we dare not reveal the things that we vaguely know to be true about ourselves. All too often in secular society we find people talking about loneliness but not knowing how to deal with it. Or, if they are aware of how to deal with it, they find themselves impotent to do so.

The Church, on the other hand, ought to be the place in which people begin to find God's answer for them in terms of a deep, loving, meaningful, relationship with the significant others in their lives. But in the Church, sadly enough, we find people either denying their loneliness because it seems to them to be somehow "unchristian" or pretending to be better than they are and shutting the door to meaningful relationships based on honesty and transparency.

No one is more lonely than two Christians living together or working side by side and pretending to be better than they are. Some of the most astonishing miracles I have seen have occurred when Christians have stopped playing games and dared to appropriate the power that God has made available in Christ. Because of this power, they have dared to love each other enough to reveal those things about themselves that could be threatening or damaging.

To illustrate this kind of miracle, let me tell you about the marriage of two people whom I have known intimately for decades now. By varying the circumstances and personalities just a bit, I could make this my own story or that of literally dozens of other people I know. What happened to this couple, John and Alice, is far from an isolated incident. It is typical of those who have heard the good news that in Christ they need no longer be strangers to themselves or to their spouses.

The miracle that happened to John and Alice can be gleaned from reading excerpts from letters they wrote to me shortly after I had spent three days visiting in their home at the time of a conference focused on small groups and the witness of the laity.

First Alice wrote, "How I wish you were sitting here in my kitchen as you were last Thursday morning. My heart is so full of love and thankfulness that I can scarcely write. If you could see me, you would understand. Except that God spoke through you that morning, you could not have known so clearly what I needed to challenge me to stir me out of my ineffectual spiritual life. I was hungering to grow more fully so that God could use me more effectively to help others. Somehow I always knew that one day I would have to be honest with John, but I needed a challenge such as you gave me that day.

"On Thursday evening, just a couple of hours after you said goodbye to us, I paid the price. The fear I have carried for fifteen years was released in a few minutes as I spoke the truth to John about my past life. I prayed that he would understand, but I never thought the results could be so wonderful. God has blessed me beyond my worthiness with a man who loves me more now in spite of knowing the truth. Truly this has been a miracle of His great concern and love for a penitent sinner such as me.

"For the first time in my life I feel like a real, whole person, free of myself, forgiven and accepted by God and by the wonderful man He has given me to love in this life. My love for John has taken on an exciting new depth and meaning such as I've never before experienced. I am free to love him instead of trying to make up to him for my past by pretending; free to admit my failures without fear of losing his love; and even free to disagree with him and lose my temper—which I seldom permitted myself to do before. Free of the need to wear a mask before my family and friends. I feel so released and grateful it is hard to express my joy.

"It's been five days since that encounter, and instead of losing this peaceful glow, I sense a deeper presence of Christ in my life each day. I know that days of spiritual dryness will come, but I thank God for graciously granting me this time of complete joy and peace.

"On Friday I had an opportunity to speak with a woman who is having a lot of marital discord. For the first time, God gave me love and understanding for this person who has always been so difficult. Although the time wasn't right to speak out completely, I did say enough to shatter her ideas of me with my former holier-than-thou attitudes. What great lengths I used to go to in order to create the impression that 'Alice never has any problems, troubles or temptations!'

"Because I had been completely honest with John, a second miracle occurred the following night when we took a long walk under the glory of God's starlit heavens. John was honest with me. Even though his past was not nearly as black as mine, this brought him a release, too. He wants to tell you that part himself, one day soon."

The following day I received a letter from John in which he did just that.

"As Alice has indicated, on Thursday night we sat side by side in the dark and she told me about her talk with you, her wrestling with the problem previously, and her need to discuss it with me.

"What happened before our marriage is of absolutely no consequence to me. As a matter of fact, I did not want to hear the details. I truthfully feel that there was nothing to be gained by her telling it. She was willing; that's the important thing. Maybe this is my weakness—I didn't want to hear!

"However, when Alice discussed conditions since our marriage, I was crushed. How it hurt my pride to realize that she had fooled me. I recalled my conversation with you of the previous night, when I had complacently stated how happy our marriage was. Truly, I was crest-fallen.

"My love for Alice was not diminished. I felt fooled, confused, regret-ful, many mixed emotions, but through it all was the strong thread that I too had something I should confess to her. I admitted this to Alice but could not force myself to do it. I didn't want to hurt her just because she had wounded my pride. We prayed together, asking God's help and thanking Him for His blessings and Alice's release.

"Next evening we went for a walk and I was compelled to tell Alice about a condition in my life of which I was ashamed, and which has helped cloud the presence of Christ for me. I was somewhat surprised to find that this was not news to Alice; she knows me better than I know myself. But it was good to be able to tell her, good to know that there is nothing we can't talk to each other about.

"We look forward to many ups and downs, praising God for the high spots and seeking His guidance during the lows. I pray the lows will be leveled off, but I hope there are always highs such as this last week to show us how gracious our Lord is and how He reaches all of us, even the unworthy ones."

As a friend and confidante of these two and an observer of the witness their life together has been to a great many people, I can say that this experience of theirs has deepened and strengthened over the years. It has lasted.

The dynamics of what happened to John and Alice are clear. Each carried a secret in marriage. Each, out of a misplaced kind of love, was concealing something dark—one in the present and one in the past. When Alice dared to speak out about her secret, John was temporarily crushed, but later able to reveal his secret. At last these two discovered what marriage is all about. The walls came down, and they not only experienced the truth of what they had known before, that God loved them, but also experienced God's love in each other and His acceptance through the incarnation of each other's acceptance.

These dynamics are not, I think, exclusively Christian. They operate in all good marriage counseling and psychotherapy in one form or another. But I do suggest that such a step is so terribly threatening for most of us that unless we know God is for us and that we are forgiven and empowered by His Holy Spirit, we may never take such a drastic and dramatic step. And we may continue to live in a world of shadows and concealment, growing further and further away from the ones we love. It is a first or a fresh discovery of God's grace in Christ that enables a breaking down of barriers, a diminishing of loneliness, and a realization that in marriage we need no longer be strangers.

The same situation can exist between parents and children, if we hide things from one another and grow farther and farther apart. One of the great miracles of my own life is my relationship with my older son. He is a wonderful man by now and a beloved friend, but in his teen-age years he had a problem father. I nagged and criticized and tried to straighten him out because I saw in him an arrogance, smugness, and superiority that I thought needed correcting.

But the more I corrected Peter, the more aloof, withdrawn, and superior he became. Or, at least, so it seemed to me.

Then one day I was working at home and went to Peter's room to look for some paper. In his desk I discovered a poem that he had written:

Hello out there, world;
It's me in here.
Can't you see me?
What? You're having trouble hearing me?

But I'm in here.
Yes, that's right.
Inside where?
Inside myself, of course.

The outside shell is very thick;
I'm having trouble getting out.
Who am I? You say I don't sound like myself?
That's because you've never heard me.

This other guy? Oh, he's the shell I told you about.
You say that's me?
No, I'm in here;
He's just my protection.

Protection from what?
From you, the world.
I can't be hurt here.
You see, my shell keeps you away.

You, the world, are pain.
I'm safe in here;
I will never be laughed at.
The shell? Oh, he doesn't mind laughter.

Come to think of it,
I'm comfortable in here.
Why should I leave?
Hello, world, still listening?

What's that, world?
I thought for a minute you said something.
It was a faint voice;
It sounded human, real, I thought.
I thought it was answering me.

Maybe not.
I can't hear too well inside this shell.
Well, I feel funny, sleepy,
And it's so comfortable in here, world.*

When I read this poem, I was stabbed with remorse. I realized that the boy I had been trying to subdue and humiliate was really a lonely man, just like his father.

That afternoon when Peter, who was then almost fifteen, came home from school, I told him I had found his poem.

"Did you like it?" he asked.

"I thought it was terrific. Do you mind my reading it?"

"No."

"Peter, I had no idea you were lonely like your father. Forgive me for not hearing and understanding you and relating to you as one lonely man to another."

"But, Dad, you're not lonely. You've got hundreds of friends."

"Well, Pete," I said, "it doesn't matter how many friends one has.

* "Hello, World" by Peter Larson, © 1969, Faith at Work, Inc.

There's no escape from loneliness. You wonder what would happen to those friends if the circumstances of your life would change—if you would lose the qualities other people found desirable. Friends are perhaps the greatest thing God can give you, outside of the gift of Himself, but even with friends one has deep loneliness. And I suppose the mark of a Christian is that he knows how to deal with his loneliness."

From that point, Peter and I talked about who we were as people. We talked about our needs, and about how Christians ought to be really aware of the loneliness of others in their homes. What struck me in that conversation was the enormity of our sin in being unwilling or unable to hear the silent screams of loneliness from those with whom we live.

Peter, through his poem, was able to reveal something to his father of how he felt. His vulnerability made me less critical for the time being, and able to be vulnerable as well. This was the beginning of a new relationship between two men who not only love each other but know now of their need for each other's love and friendship.

I am sure this is the mark of the good news in a Christian's life. We cannot escape loneliness, but we can make it creative as we learn to know Jesus Christ, who Himself is the man of sorrows and loneliness.

When we allow Him to enter our lives, we should become sensitive to the needs of those about us. The Body of Christ then becomes a fellowship of those who can share their loneliness and who can say to a lonely world, "Come on in. We're lonely, too, but we believe that God is here and we can know Him and one another in a deep way."

In one sense, there is an artlessness in the gift Christians have for one another in this relationship. Dr. Paul Tournier, during the seminar mentioned earlier, described the disappointment some counselors experience after visiting him in Geneva. They come to learn his methods of counseling and of enabling in the "medicine of the whole person." They go away disappointed, Dr. Tournier says, because "I have no methods. All I do is accept people."

In this artless stance of simply accepting people, we find the great, good news of the gospel. God simply accepts us in Jesus Christ; He made Himself vulnerable, loved us, and affirmed us. He calls us to love one another as He has loved us.

This is the very thing that happened when my son Peter let me know something of who he was in his loneliness. He accepted me, and when he did so I was able to open my life and accept him in return. This is the mystery and wonder of the gospel of Jesus Christ in contemporary life.

When we are able to appropriate and develop such qualities as openness, transparency, and lack of deviousness, we find that life is enhanced both in terms of our sense of well-being and in terms of our relationships with others. When we lack these qualities, we not only fail to live up to our full potential but also run the risk of damaging those we love.

A group of psychologists who did a study of schizophrenic children concluded that great damage can be done to children by parents who simultaneously communicate ambivalent emotions. For example, when a child is naughty and the parent decides to punish him or her, the parent may smile lovingly, and after saying soothing words such as, "This is going to hurt me more than it hurts you," proceeds to whale the tar out of the child. The poor youngster doesn't know whether to respond with open arms to the smile and soothing voice or to protect himself or herself against the spanking.

In the opinion of the psychologists who conducted this study, a child can handle justified punishment as well as love and approval, provided he or she is on the receiving end of a single emotion consistently acted out. But if the two are mixed, serious illness is likely to result. Phony parents, who pretend to be loving even when they are angry, can wreak havoc in the emotional lives of their children.

The point is obvious. We must not be afraid to be ourselves with our children: justifiably angry at one moment and unashamedly loving and expansive at another. It is in playing the role of an even-tempered, never angry, "Christian" parent that we do real harm. To be a genuine parent is to be able to be yourself with your children, and not someone else.

I am convinced that Christ wants to help us trust our emotions more than we do, and to guard our emotions less and less. Our emotions sometimes prompt us to honest hostility; at other times they urge us to lavish love. We seem to be afraid of both things, and so we live in a gray world and cloud the lives of our children and loved ones and even our colleagues. Samuel Butler said, "To live is like to love—all reason is against it and all healthy instinct is for it." We are most loving and most truly alive when we are our naked, vulnerable selves, lavishly affirming and honestly relating to those around us.

Some of us, when we have learned to be vulnerable, still find it difficult to be affirmative of others. We are often tempted to feel that we must take God's place and play the corrector or the "straightener-outer" of someone else, rather than to bring the word of affirmation that would really make a difference in his or her life.

Let me speak for a moment as a husband, and as one who at times cannot bear to be outwardly hostile but must play some kind of "Christian game" even in anger, and withdraw into a shell of politeness. Suppose that you are such a husband, and that for several days and nights you and your wife have been withdrawn or hostile and your physical and verbal communication has been close to zero.

Then suppose that God finally gets through to you and tells you that life is too short to live like this; that you must seize the moment and love as God loves you. It is up to you to break the stalemate. Night falls, bedtime approaches, and you decide that the time has come to reestablish communication with your wife.

As a husband, you have two choices of what to say: both true, but both only half-truths. You may smile expectantly and say with as much warmth as possible, "Dear, it's been a long time since we had any romance around here."

No matter how you say this, the message your wife hears is, "I'm keeping track, and you're not making it as a loving wife." She knows this as well as you do, and what you have said merely underscores whatever guilt she may be feeling.

On the other hand, you can say, "You know, Dear, to me you are more beautiful than the day I married you, and I love you more than ever before. You're terrific; you really turn me on."

Of course I can't guarantee the results of this approach, but chances are it will lead to some "creative dialogue!"

We have the same kind of choice in all our relationships. When we realize that the people around us are as guilty as we are, and that they don't need their guilt underscored, we can supply the word of affirmation that tells them they are loved, cared for and appreciated. Husbands need this; wives need it; children need it; even aunts, uncles and grandparents need it.

Once at a conference I was leading a seminar on the subject of broken relationships. During the final half-hour we had some creative dialogue by opening up the session to questions and answers. The last person to speak was a woman. "Can God heal a broken relationship that isn't just broken—it doesn't exist?" she asked.

When pressed for an explanation, she said, "My husband and I never quarrel and are never angry. We simply have no relationship. He comes home from work, has dinner, watches television, reads the paper, and then goes to bed. Later on, after I have read the paper and watched television, I go to bed."

"Is it like that every night?" I asked.

"Every night for years," she answered.

"Are you both Christians?"

"No. I am a Christian, but my husband is not."

"Do you love him?"

"Yes," she said, tears beginning to form in her eyes. "I love him very much."

"Do you think he loves you?"

"No, I am sure he doesn't, or he wouldn't be so cold and indifferent."

"Well," I said, "as a Christian, you are the one who must be vulnerable and find out the true nature of your husband's feelings. He must love you or he wouldn't be coming home to this dreadfully boring routine every night. He'd be out bowling or drinking or doing something a little more creative than what you describe. Perhaps he's hoping that one day something will happen to rekindle the love that you shared when you were first married."

"But what can I do?" the woman asked.

"What are you doing now to try to change the relationship?"

"I keep inviting him to our prayer group," she replied, "and I leave books and pamphlets around, hoping he will read them."

"Is this working?"

"No," she admitted.

"Then why don't you try something much more radical and costly to you? This is what the cross is all about. Why not try to be vulnerable for your husband in the same way that Christ on the cross was vulnerable for you?"

"Give me a for instance."

I grabbed at something wild. "Some night when he's watching television, why don't you put on your flimsiest lace nightie and your best perfume, jump into his lap and ruffle his hair and tell him you love him as much as ever. What do you think his response would be?"

"I'd hate to guess," she giggled.

"But what's the worst thing that might happen if you took this step in faith?"

Without a moment's hesitation, she replied, "He might laugh at me."

"That's true. And would that hurt?"

"It would hurt more than anything I can think of."

"It seems to me that this is what faith in Christ is all about, lived out in the dimension of marriage. To leave tracts and pamphlets around and to suggest that your husband come to your prayer group really makes you superior and invulnerable. But to do something like this gives him the chance to respond lovingly or with indifference. Do you have enough faith in Christ to enable you to take such a risk?"

A few days later, back at my office, I got this letter:
"Dear Bruce, I did what you suggested and guess what? He didn't laugh!"

It was the beginning of a new relationship between the two of them. Of course it might not have turned out so happily. The point is that we Christians need to realize that in living out the dynamics of the gospel we must become radically vulnerable and radically affirmative to those with whom we live.

Certainly this will be costly, and we will often fail. But apart from this kind of radical behavior, there is sometimes no way in which God can work through us to build some deep relationships with the significant others in our lives.

Samuel Johnson once wrote, "Marriage has many pains, but celibacy has no pleasures." I'd like to paraphrase this for the Christian, married or single: "This radical style of life in Christ has many pains, but anything less has few pleasures." The more we guard our lives and the more we protect ourselves, the more lonely and withdrawn we become. As we discover in Jesus Christ both the example we need and the power to live as He lived, we go through the pain into a life of deep, loving relationships. Through this kind of radical obedience we discover that we are no longer strangers.

A friend of mine, a devout Christian and a successful businessman, once revealed a bit of his background that helped to explain how he became the person he is today. He said that throughout his childhood, he would often hear his Scottish father repeat this bit of philosophy:

The time to be happy is now;
The place to be happy is here;
The way to be happy is to make other people happy.

I believe in that philosophy. The only thing it fails to include is the dynamic, which is Jesus Christ Himself.

Heaven begins here. If it doesn't begin here, it doesn't begin at all. The people we live with now and the circumstances we live in are the very stuff of the new life in Christ. The way to be happy is to make other people happy by living a Christian style—that is, one of vulnerability and affirmation. This opens us to the possibility of relationships and lets others find happiness in discovering a relationship with us.

No one says that it is easy to be affirmative. Sometimes, in pointing out the difficulty of an affirmative stance, we point to the evidence in Scripture that Jesus Himself became angry. It seems to me, however, as

I read the New Testament, that Jesus' anger was always directed against attitudes, conditions, or groups—never against individuals.

He railed against the Pharisees, yes; but not against the individual Nicodemus, who was a Pharisee. Immorality in any form made Him angry, it is true; but when confronted with a single woman taken in adultery, Jesus showed only love and compassion and affirmation. Our Lord vented His anger against those who dishonored God and took advantage of people by trafficking in the temple, but when he encountered Zacchaeus, a tax collector who was a notorious cheat, His approach could hardly have been more affirmative.

We can learn from this. At home, at work, in our communities, or as citizens of a nation, we can take a stand against groups that are destructive. We can and should become angry about unfair conditions and immorality and fight them with all the means at our disposal. But in relating to an individual within a structure, whatever it may be, the only course open to us, if we are to love as Jesus loved, is to affirm that person in his or her worth, uniqueness, beauty, and in the very real gifts and strengths he may have which are still hidden.

Sometimes it is especially difficult for Christians to practice their faith in terms of affirmation toward a member of the family. When this is the case, God in His amazing love may use someone outside the family circle to bring the needed word of affirmation.

In our family we saw a vivid illustration of this when our younger son, Mark, was in elementary school. For a number of years, Mark had difficulty with the whole learning process, and his parents and older brother and sister seemed to focus only on his faults and failings. We tried to scold and shame and goad him into becoming a better student.

When Mark got to the fifth grade, something unusual happened. He began to bring home papers with marks far higher than they seemed to warrant. Complimentary comments were written in the margins. I thought his teacher was failing to do her job because she seemed to be giving more credit than was due.

When parents' back-to-school night came, I went to see the teacher with the idea of straightening her out and urging this young woman, who was new at teaching, to be more judicious in her grading. But after spending an evening in the classroom with her, I realized that she genuinely liked and appreciated little boys in the fifth grade who were messy, not too punctual, and who did not seem to have a great scholastic interest.

And what happened to Mark in his year under the affirmative guidance of that teacher was nothing less than a miracle, for which I will always thank God. The learning process was changed for him—or, rather, he was changed for the learning process. I believe that God used that remarkable teacher to minister in the tradition of affirmation in a situation where parents had failed.

Some friends of ours who have a marked ability to love and affirm people had great difficulty a few years back in affirming their own teenage sons. The mother was a staff worker in the local church, and she and her husband wanted their two boys to participate in the dynamic youth program of the congregation. But the boys preferred to associate with a black-leather-jacket motorcycle crowd. Needless to say, the parents openly disapproved.

One day, while taking part in a small group discussion, the mother was challenged. She had been complaining that God had given her a tremendous love for her children, but that it hadn't made any difference in their behavior. Someone asked her if she loved her boys in a way that *they* could understand. At first she said yes, but after thinking more about it, she decided that was probably not true. Instead, she had loved them in ways meaningful to her.

Then she was challenged to think of a way she could let her sons know in unmistakable terms that they were loved just as they were. Quickly, she came up with the ridiculous notion that to love them meant to accept and love their friends, and even to invite them into her home.

As an act of faith, she did this, and it transformed the relationship between the parents and their two rebellious children.

Parenthetically, the leader of the motorcycle crowd later came into contact with a dynamic interdenominational youth ministry, in which he found Christ, and he in turn brought the older son of my friends to a commitment to Jesus Christ. Through this experience the parents entered into a redemptive relationship with their sons at the point of affirming them where they were. The lesson is that by criticizing and withholding blessing and affirmation, we may rob those close to us of a possible discovery of God's love for them in Jesus Christ.

One further illustration may help to shed light on what can happen to an intimate relationship when the power of God breaks through in a fresh way. This illustration, in the form of a letter from a minister who had attended a clergy conference, speaks for itself. It says more in concrete terms than one could hope to say in abstractions. The writer begins his letter by telling about his own tremendous release which resulted from accepting himself in a small group of Christian ministers who dared to be honest, affirmative, and vulnerable. He then goes on to tell about returning home to join his wife, who had just come back from a similar conference: "When she returned on Friday, I had tried to prepare myself by recognizing that very significant things were happening to her in that conference. And for the first time in our nine years of marriage, I was not part of this significant happening in her life. But nothing could have prepared me for the hurt of her telling me almost immediately on her return, 'I have had some of the most significant relationships of my life this week, and I met some men, one in particular, with whom I shared more meaningfully in every way—except sexually—than I have ever shared with you.'

"I wanted to vomit—to break out in a dead run and never stop. Somehow by sheer grace I did neither, and heard myself saying, 'You know, don't you, that I have overshadowed you in our nine years of marriage, and have never let you be a person. I want to tell you today that I am very, very sorry.'

"She told how one of the men had picked her out to relate the story of his hurt life. And I could only respond in honesty, 'I've never told you the story of my life because I was afraid of hurting you and destroying our relationship.'

"She said, 'But this is what I have needed you to do. I've needed you to need me.'

"We talked for two hours before supper. I had a wedding to perform after supper, but we scheduled two more hours before bedtime and woke up in the middle of the night and talked for at least two hours more.

"During most of this time I was pouring out my life's story to her, especially those things about which I had always felt guilty before and after our marriage. And I tried to tell her everything that I was afraid of. I shared with her the things that happened to me at the clergy conference, repeating some of my conversation with you when you told me about how you and your wife found help in recognizing that you could not meet all of each other's needs.

"It is now Monday after that Friday, and this is still a very fresh wound. We are negotiating the whole emotional climate of our marriage. We have agreed to come to each other with our hurts for the rest of our married life. Looking back, we see that our primary mistake was not being willing to share with each other those things that really hurt us most. For nine years we thought our relationship was pretty good until we got a look at it.

"It's still pretty recent that all this broke. I'm painfully aware that we both have risked our entire relationship, but I think we are going to make it, and when we do, it will be amid shouts of pain and joy.

"Do you remember my smugly telling you that my best relationship was with my six-year-old boy, perhaps because he didn't threaten me? You said that someday he would hurt me because of my love for him. I want you to know that my best relationship is *not* with my son, although it is pretty good. My best relationship is with my wife, and I didn't have any idea—no idea!—how much I loved her until she hurt me deeply."

I think this says it all. It says that at the heart of the gospel there are two things: a cross and celebration. The cross implies vulnerability, God's for us, and ours for others. When we walk through the cross into the light, we find that the very good news of the gospel has to do with celebration—a celebration of the fact that we are no longer strangers.

You and the World

Jesus Christ does not tell us to "take Him into the world." Rather, He calls us to come into the world because we belong to Him, and to discover that He is already there in the dispossessed, the lonely, the repressed, and depressed. By moving into the world we find that He is there, eager to meet us, and we discover anew that we need no longer be strangers in the world which Christ created and for which He gave Himself as a sacrifice. Our destiny is in the world with Christ.

7

You and the World

A wise man once said that every Christian needs two conversions: one out of the world and a second back into the world.

No Christian will question the need to be converted from the world, if by "the world," we mean false values, immorality, and the worship of material things. Traditionally, Christians have viewed the world as the arena in which they give their witness to the resurrection of Christ, to the love of God, and to the power of the Holy Spirit, all the while trying to remain uncorrupted by the forces of evil which the world represents and embodies. Yet this stance has often given Christians a strange posture and a somewhat detached attitude. We might call it the "prophetic" stance, for I suppose evangelism has usually been seen as the New Testament form of the prophetic, with John the Baptist as its foremost symbol.

Only recently have we come to see the need for Christians to be converted back into the world, which may very well have been in the mind of Christ from the beginning. Although the world needs the witness and service of the Christian, the Christian needs the world even more.

Why? Because the world is the arena in which we find our true being. Jesus Christ is in the world, waiting to reveal Himself to the Christian—waiting to complete the Christian as a person.

In this view, the world is not an alien place which the Christian plunges into, much as a diver plunges to the bottom of the sea wearing a pressurized suit and having a long airhose connecting him to the life-giving atmosphere above. Rather, we Christians find ourselves in the world naturally, and in the world we find Jesus Christ. We have no other arena in which to operate. It is futile to attempt to remove ourselves from the world, thinking that we will find some rarefied spiritual atmo-sphere more congenial to our calling as Christians.

The message of the New Testament is crystal clear on this point. We love Christ and serve Him by loving and serving people. Jesus said that inasmuch as we have done it (shown mercy) unto one of the least of these, we have done it unto Him. When we feed the hungry, clothe the naked, share someone's burden, visit a prisoner, heal the sick, free the enslaved, give comfort to the dying, we do it for Christ and to Christ. This is inescapable if we take the Scriptures seriously. How, then, have so many of us dodged the true import of this call and obligation?

One of the exciting things happening today is the rediscovery of this essential fact, that for the Christian to be a whole person he must be at home in the world.

To be at home in the world does not mean to sell out, to conform to shoddy standards, or to settle for something less than the best that God has in mind for us. It simply means that we can apply the principles of a Christian style of life in this area, and establish a meaningful relation-ship with the world wherever we find goodness, morality, strength, love, light, or hope, and we are to become vulnerable to the world insofar as we see our own needs, weakness, and loneliness. Reduced to absolute basics, we are to love the world even as our Lord loves the world.

The importance of this truth was brought home to me several years ago when my stepfather died. My mother was a remarkable Christian and had been since childhood, but she had a hard time accepting my step-father's death. Loneliness, grief, and many other emotions assailed her, and she was quite unstrung.

Members of the family and friends offered to stay with Mother until she could adjust to her new situation, but as a Christian, she maintained that Jesus Christ was adequate for her needs. She refused help and said that she would not accept the consolation of visitors or a roommate to share her apartment until Christ Himself gave her the strength and hope and help she needed to carry on.

Months went by, and Mother's grief and loneliness continued. All the while she maintained her steadfast commitment to Christ, involvement in the life of the church, weekly worship, participation in a small Bible study group, and leadership in the missionary society of her congregation. She also read her Bible and prayed morning and night. None of this was enough.

Finally, one of the pastors in Mother's church asked her to help in a new program offering tutoring to some grade school children in a nearby black ghetto in Chicago. As a former teacher, she accepted this assignment, though she was decades older than most of the volunteer tutors, and she was assigned a fifth-grader named Rosemary. Mother began to tutor Rosemary on a regular basis and to become involved with her.

Almost immediately I saw a change in my mother; her friends, too, noticed this change. She found a channel for her love and a renewed experience of what it meant to be needed and to give of herself sacrificially to another human being. It was through Rosemary that God gave her the promised consolation, help, and strength that she needed to bear her loneliness and grief as a widow.

We can say that God sent my mother to Rosemary as an expression of His love and concern for that little girl. But we can also say that God sent Rosemary to my mother. Through this child, Christ ministered to Mother and set her free of the pain that the death of a spouse can give.

This underlined for me the fact that we Christians need more than worship and prayer and Bible study and a genuinely pious life. We need also to be involved in the world and its needs, not only for the world's sake but for our own. Only in this kind of involvement can we become whole people, discovering Christ and being ministered to by Him.

What God did for my mother through Rosemary is but one example of what happens to Christians who come out of their shells and become personally involved in meeting the needs of a suffering world. Amazing things happen to those who see opportunities for service and respond to them in whatever limited, amateurish ways are at their disposal. Feelings of inadequacy or the sense that we are faced with insuperable problems should not discourage us from tackling whatever is at hand—whatever we are equipped to handle with whatever resources are ours. What is more, we usually find that our capabilities exceed our original estimation of them. When we are faithful, God supplies power far beyond our most generous expectations.

I think of Bob, a friend of mine, a clergyman about my age, who has taught me a great deal about the life of service and compassion. He stepped into a new dimension of wholeness when he was drafted by a committee of citizens to run for mayor of his suburban town. This community is wracked by all kind of typical urban/suburban problems, and to serve as its mayor is pretty much a thankless task. Yet Bob sought the dollar-a-year post, after much prayer and with the encouragement and support of a small group of close Christian friends.

As mayor he was not able to bring about miracles, to turn a problem-wracked city into near Utopia. Yet I am convinced that God sent my friend to help lead his community in a time of growth and transition and change. In just as profound a way, Bob discovered Christ anew through assuming the responsibilities implicit in being mayor of an active suburban town.

Of course, we cannot all run for office, any more than we can all tutor disadvantaged children. But in terms of our own place of power and influence, we can become sensitized to the world's needs and begin to respond to them for Christ's sake. Certainly there is much in the world that needs to be changed. On every hand we see brutality, loneliness, and man's manipulation and use of other men for his own purposes. If, through fear, distaste, or a misguided kind of spirituality, we close our eyes to the world's needs and our ears to its cries for help, we will have failed miserably as disciples of Him who loved the world and died for it.

It is not difficult to affirm the world when we begin to become involved with people outside the Christian sphere of influence, and even outside a commitment to Christ. The world is not a good place, but there is much good in it, which we can discover if we open our eyes.

One day I was riding in a bus down Michigan Avenue in Chicago when an advertising poster attracted my attention. It was not a commercial message, and there was no indication of who had placed the ad in the bus. This is what it said:

My worth is not adequately recognized. Send a signal of fellow-feeling.

Today I did a foolish, embarrassing thing. Send a signal of shared chagrin.

My self-esteem is willing to trample yours. Send a signal of forgiveness.

I am alone in a selfish, disinterested world. Send a signal of mutual humanity.

To receive the mind of Christ is to hear the world saying just such words. Whatever else the world may be, it is lonely, hungry, guilty, and eager to make contact with a human being who will listen and understand, accept and love. The Christian ought to be just this kind of person. He ought to affirm that those outside of Christ have worth, uniqueness, and significance. The Christian can then affirm all of the deep desires and longings that are in the world, call them good, and respond as a fellow human to a fellow human.

Jesus Christ Himself is the pattern of this new kind of being turned loose in the world. We who belong to Christ ought to follow His example of love and affirmation for those who are outside the Kingdom, hoping that some will be affirmed to such a degree that they will themselves discover Christ and God's love in Christ, and thereby step inside the Kingdom.

Instead, it seems to me, we tend to emulate John the Baptist, calling down wrath and doom upon a lonely, lost society. Jesus loved John, to be sure, and called him the greatest of those born among women—but He added that John was "the least in the Kingdom of God."

It is easy to castigate the world, to catalogue its sins. Easy, yes, and it doesn't cost us a thing. But Jesus Christ calls us to do the costly thing: to speak the word of love and affirmation for His sake.

For all too many years, I commuted into New York from my home in New Jersey. At one point I changed from a Central Railroad of New Jersey train to a Path train, which is simply a subway connecting the two states. One day, squeezing into the overflowing car, I was shocked and astonished to hear a warm and friendly voice coming over the loud-speaker system, "Good morning! Welcome to the Path railroad!"

Those who live in the metropolitan New York area, and those who have visited recently, will realize how shocking it was to hear a warm and friendly greeting on a subway train.

I cannot remember all that the conductor said, but he was truly a pastor to a worried, harried, hurried bunch of commuters rushing into Manhattan. He had a friendly greeting at each stop, and as people left the train, he would open his window and call out a personal word to various ones whom he had come to know during his tour of duty on that line.

I could not resist going over and talking to that man. He told me that several years before he had had a real change in his life which had altered his whole life style. Here was a man who was loving and caring for people as he daily conducted commuters into New York City. Certainly his witness has not been in vain.

The new creature in Christ, whether he be a brain surgeon, a teacher, a farmer, or a subway conductor, ought to be one who can affirm the people who cross his path or who partake of the services which he offers. I wonder how many people have spoken to that conductor, as I did, commenting on his friendly attitude and giving him the opportunity to bear witness to the source and motivation of his life style.

But if the world needs to see Christians who are affirmative, it also needs to see those who are vulnerable. This is the other side of the coin of the Christian style.

Jesus Himself could reveal His needs and hopes and fears to those about Him. He was free to ask Zacchaeus for a meal and to ask a Samaritan woman of questionable morality for a drink of water. He was free to ask for the ministry of comfort and consolation from three of His disciples on the night before His crucifixion. "Come with me into the garden and keep me company," He asked, "while I pray and wrestle through the will of God for me as I face tomorrow and all it may hold."

This was the Lord of heaven and earth, speaking in all His vulnerable humanity. What does it say to us who seek to minister in His name? All too often we have hidden our loneliness, hurts, and hungers from other people—afraid that if we let them know that we struggle as they do, we will fail to uphold God's reputation!

Nothing could be further from the pattern Jesus gave us. In point of fact, authentic leadership involves sharing your troubles with people and thus encouraging them in their struggles. The Christian who wants to provide leadership must be willing to acknowledge his own growing edge: his needs, loneliness, or failures as a Christian.

Let yourself imagine this situation: a pastor calls several of the key lay people in his church and invites them over on a Saturday night. "I am putting the coffee pot on," he says. "I need company tonight as I wrestle through God's plan and purpose for my life. I haven't prayed in ten days. I've been rude to my wife and neglected my children. I have no authentic message from God for my people tomorrow. Yet I believe that God loves me and that He can change and transform me to get me out of this alienated state. Tonight I'm going to pray. Will you come keep me company and pray with me and help me?"

Think about such a situation for a moment. Think about what might happen to such a pastor and his friends and the entire church. Then think about the alternative: the pastor struggling alone, remaining aloof and invulnerable and trying to make it on his own.

This imaginary situation shocks us because it is so atypical—but it should be typical! Even within the church, "the company of the committed," vulnerability is a rare commodity, yet it is in becoming vulnerable that Christians find mutual help and wholeness.

Perhaps it is within the Church then that we should learn how to become vulnerable, and we can then make the transfer which will allow us to become vulnerable to the world in a life-producing way. As I travel about the nation, I find men and women everywhere who have succeeded in "making the transfer" and who are witnessing by word and deed to their colleagues in the secular world.

An example of this kind of lay person is a medical doctor whom I met several years ago. An Episcopal rector and his wife had invited me to dine with them, and the doctor was also their guest. During the course of the evening, the clergyman asked the doctor about the progress of a certain child who was convalescing at the hospital where the doctor worked. The reply was that the child was making a remarkable recovery, and the two men then went on to exchange a few words about the power of prayer and the number of groups in the parish praying for the recovery of the child.

When the doctor was asked if he had told his colleagues at the hospital, who were baffled by the child's physical recovery, what he thought was the source of the present-day miracle, he seemed to be embarrassed. "No," he said, "I guess I'm afraid. I don't think they would understand."

This intrigued me, and I asked the doctor if he ever bore witness o his faith in Christ to his medical colleagues.

"Oh, yes," he said, "I do this frequently."

"What sort of thing do you say?"

"Well," he replied, "I tell them that marvelous things have begun to happen to me in terms of my marriage. And I tell them of my own failures and of how Jesus Christ is giving me a new love and a new relationship with my teen-age children."

Then I realized that the doctor had been guided by God to lead from weakness, not from strength. If he had told his colleagues about the prayer groups backing up his medical ministry, he would have threatened them and turned them off. But by speaking of his own needs as a man, he enabled them to identify with him and at the same time to become aware of the hope that he had and of the grace of God operating in his life.

When I realized this, I told the doctor that I thought he was being led of the Spirit in his witness to his teammates at the hospital. He laughed and thanked me for saying it, adding that he often thought of himself as a coward.

Then he went on to share with us an experience that he had never before revealed. One of his patients, a personal friend, had undergone surgery and was in the hospital's intensive care unit. The patient's heart stopped beating, and when the surgeon got the message, he rushed to his friend's bedside, finding that the emergency team was already there trying to bring the man back to life. But the machine monitoring the function of the patient's heart revealed that he was dead.

Deeply saddened because he had lost both a patient and a friend, the surgeon turned to leave the room. Suddenly he felt an urge to go back and pray. He had never done this before, but he acted on his impulse. Unnoticed by the others in the room, he stood at the foot of the bed, placed his hand upon the foot of the patient, and said a simple prayer, "Jesus, bless this child of yours, my friend John."

The moment he said this prayer, he noticed on the machine that the man's heart had begun to beat again. Subsequently the patient recovered.

Now, the doctor had enough wisdom and guidance from God so that he never told his colleagues that he had witnessed a modern miracle, not unlike the raising of Lazarus. Had he shared something of this event, which really ought to be reported to the Christian community alone, he would have closed doors and limited his own witness. Instead, he witnessed out of his own need and vulnerability as a man. And later, the rector told me something of how many people the surgeon had influenced for Jesus Christ in the course of his daily life.

This story is a good illustration of the attitude we Christians must take if we are to make an impression on the world in line with our Lord's example and strategy. To approach our fellowmen outside the family of faith with an attitude of superiority, power, and extraordinary wisdom will only put them off and diminish the possibility of leading them into a relationship with Christ. But to share our common humanity in an open, vulnerable way is to approach the ideal of servanthood which should be the goal of all Christians in their relationship to the world.

Very simply, Christians are told to love the world. God so loved the world that He gave His only-begotten Son. Christ did not die for the Church; He died for the world because He loved the world. The Church is made up of those who are called to be a part of Christ, that He might live in us and that His love for the world might be incarnated in us and through us for the world's sake.

The key word on the lips of those who are concerned for the world is *involvement.* We must be involved in the struggles, hopes, fears, needs of the world. This means politically involved, socially involved, psychologically involved. The fact that we belong to Christ does not excuse us from our responsibility to minister to the world's needs in these various areas.

In fact, as Christians, we should be especially sensitive to the tasks and problems at hand and particularly concerned to do our part in meeting needs and solving problems.

Recalling Martin Luther's advice that we are to "love God and sin boldly," we may interpret this further to declare that we believe enough in grace so that we are not afraid to be involved, or fearful that some of the world's meanness or ugliness or dishonesty will rub off on us. Becoming involved will open the door to our being touched by the world's sin. There is no way to avoid it. But again, the Christian is not someone who is afraid of sin and the guilt that results from sin.

Our witness to the world is that we are free enough to be totally involved, because we know God's answer for both sin and guilt. We know the good news; we are forgiven. We need no longer be strangers to the world, for we have a sense of security, a place to stand, that comes from belonging to God and that enables us to become the most completely involved men and women of our time.

When we try to separate ourselves from the world in the wrong sense, we declare that above all we must keep ourselves clean and pure. By indirection, this implies that we do not have a God whose love and forgiveness are adequate for us.

On the other hand, when we become deeply involved, we speak to the world about a God whose grace is unlimited and boundless and all-encompassing. We bear witness most to the love of Christ by our own freedom to become involved and our lack of fear of what this involvement may do to us.

Think about it for a moment and you cannot escape the conclusion that those Christians who seem to make the greatest impression on the world, and incidentally become heroes within the family of faith, are those who take great risks, brave real dangers, become totally involved with those whom they serve in Christ's name, and disregard the consequences. Those who piously remove themselves from the mainstream of life, either out of fear or distaste or out of the need to be spiritually superior, have missed the point of the gospel. And they have missed the fulfilling adventure of authentic Christianity.

If you are wondering where and how to begin, the answer is to begin where you are with whatever needs you see.

One man who did this is Keith Leenhouts of Royal Oak, Michigan. As a young man, he became a judge in the misdemeanant court of his suburban community, and he was overwhelmed by the enormity of the problems he saw in his capacity as a judge. Most of the offenders who came into Judge Leenhouts' court were teen-agers. The judge was reluctant simply to dismiss their cases, since they had broken laws, but neither did he want to send them to prison where they would be exposed to hardened criminals.

At last he went to a psychiatrist friend of his, described a typical case, and asked for advice. The case involved a young man who had stolen a car, drunk too much, and smashed up the car.

What to do about this youthful offender baffled Judge Leenhouts. The psychiatrist was not able to give him much encouragement. After studying the dossier on the case and interviewing the boy, he said, "Judge, I'm afraid there's nothing I can do for this young man. He has what we call a character disorder. He acts on impulse without regard for the consequences."

The judge then asked, "Isn't there some medical treatment or psychiatric treatment or some process in social work that will change a young man like this?"

"Not really," was the answer. "And it's not an unusual situation. Eighty-five percent of those who come before your court will be people with character disorders."

"What will I do?" asked the judge.

"You have to insert into their lives inspiring personalities. Punishment alone won't change people. They must be shown a better way to live through contact with other persons."

The more Judge Leenhouts thought about this dilemma, the more concerned he became to do something about it. As a Christian, he believed that God had some kind of plan that could be discovered to rehabilitate lost people.

He asked eight of his friends, including the psychiatrist, to help him establish a new program for the rehabilitation of misdemeanants with character disorders. Some of these friends had psychological or theological training but others did not. Nevertheless, when these eight men began to act as sponsors for youngsters in trouble with the law and to become their friends and confidantes, results began to be seen. Positive changes took place in the lives of youngsters who would otherwise have been shunted aside into jail or set free to get into further trouble.

Judge Leenhouts went to more and more people in Royal Oak asking for volunteers who would simply love, affirm, and become involved with young people in trouble. Eventually, more than five hundred individuals in the city were involved in the program and the rate of rehabilitation among the youthful offenders in Judge Leenhouts' court more than tripled.

God had revealed a new way to use the untapped resources of His people in the Church to deal with a growing problem in our nation for which experts in the field of penology had no answer. Today, Keith Leenhouts heads up a nationwide program of harnessing the power of the laity to help rehabilitate young people.

It seems to me that this dramatizes what the Christian stance is to be. The Christian is to believe that no one is hopeless and that God has a plan for everyone, no matter how sick or distorted his life may be. We must believe that God loves the world and wants to change it; that He wants to free and redeem individuals, and that we can become participants with Him in his thrilling adventure. To do this means that we will perpetually find new ways by which God is at work to liberate individuals and groups.

For Christians of an evangelical or conservative persuasion, a new door is opening. We can discover Jesus Christ in a more complete way as we discover the world. It is in the world that God has secrets to reveal to some of us that will never be revealed in a prayer group or a worship service. The latter, of course, will always be needed, nor do I mean to imply that they are less important today than ever before. But a Christian is called by his Lord to be at home in the world as much as he is at home with God, with himself, or with the community of the faithful.

The cry is often heard today that the Church has become irrelevant. What is usually meant by this is that churches seem less concerned about human problems than they were in former generations. Despite all this talk of irrelevance, there is abundant evidence that troubled individuals and disadvantaged and oppressed groups still regard the Church as a source of mercy and help.

At times the evidence of this appears to be a very backhanded compliment indeed. I still remember an incident in which a large convocation of Lutherans in Minneapolis was confronted with a group of angry, militant, highly articulate American Indians who savagely indicted the churches for failing to give help and support to the remnants of the original Americans, who—let us be honest—have been treated very shabbily for generations, sometimes brutalized, and often totally ignored. Part of the demand of this group of Indian spokesmen was for a colossal amount of money in "reparations" for bad treatment by the majority of American citizens through their government and its agencies.

The Lutheran laymen and clergymen attending this meeting reacted in a variety of ways: shock, dismay, disbelief, righteous indignation, compassion, understanding, the desire to "do something," anger, hostility.

The most interesting aspect of all this for me was the fact that a group of people who felt mistreated and ignored *turned to the church for mercy and help.* Beyond their rhetoric, beyond their demands for reparation, beyond their anger and vindictiveness, was a sincere cry for help. All of which suggests that the church—despite all charges of irrelevance—is still seen as a source of justice and mercy and committed to right.

Faced with situations like these, how do we respond? As individuals, we perhaps feel helpless and confused, yet we know that our churches, as institutions, have enormous resources and tremendous power. How the institutional church reacts and acts will depend on the reactions and actions of individuals within the institution. One thing is perfectly clear: we have a mandate from the Lord of the Church to meet human needs for His sake and in His name. This mandate is inescapable. If we wait to act until we know exactly what to do and feel certain of the righteousness of our actions, it will be too late.

We experienced this dilemma in microcosm on many occasions in our family. Like any Christian family, we have problems and we try desperately hard at times to love one another with Christ's love. Sometimes we succeed and sometimes we fail. But we turned a corner in our insight when my wife accepted a volunteer assignment to work three days a week in a Headstart program. Our children were still young and she accepted this assignment fully aware that there were still all sorts of needs and unresolved situations at home. Had she waited until everything was perfect, she would have waited forever. And by daring to move into the world, along with other women from our church, and to assume responsibility for a few preschool children with emotional problems, she discovered Jesus Christ in a new way.

There were fringe benefits for the entire family. Sitting around the dinner table in the evening and listening to my wife talk about what had happened that day, we came to know the children and the other volunteer teachers in this marvelous ministry. By participating with my wife in this ministry to the world, we were all drawn closer together and we all found something new of the nature of our Lord.

Had she neglected this opportunity that Christ gave to her through this dimension of the church's outreach, not only would a few children have been deprived of the loving ministry of a mature and sensitive woman, but our family would have been deprived of the new kind of love that comes when even one member ventures forth into the world to become involved, to affirm the potential of others, and to be vulnerable.

Jesus Christ does not tell us to "take Him into the world." Rather, He calls us to come into the world because we belong to Him, and to discover that He is already there in the dispossessed, the lonely, the repressed, and depressed. By moving into the world we find that He is there, eager to meet us, and we discover anew that we need no longer be strangers in the world which Christ created and for which He gave Himself as a sacrifice. Our destiny is in the world with Christ.

A New Church
for a New Day

The emerging Church will not be much concerned about religion. This is as it should be, for Jesus Himself didn't seem to care much for religion. He was constantly being attacked by the religious people of His day because of His attitude toward religious customs and traditions. In Jesus we see a great difference between "being religious" and knowing the Father and doing His will. Our relationship to God, made possible by Jesus Christ, and our relationships to one another become the focus and concern of the new Church. Religious trappings have had their day.

8

A New Church
for a New Day

A strangely sad mood enveloped me one Sunday morning as I sat in church next to my son and his best buddy. We were singing a hymn that has great meaning for me, a hymn written almost two centuries ago. As I lustily worshiped my Lord in song (had my wife been there, I'm sure she would have punched me and whispered, "Not so loud; you're flat!"), I glanced at my two young companions and was surprised at their obvious restraint in singing. Normally they were not restrained in anything!

Why were they so unmoved by this great hymn of the Church? I began to study it and sensed at once that the words must seem like a foreign language to them—like Chaucer or Shakespeare. The choice of words, the phrases, the very concepts spoke of a former age. Even the tune was like nothing we hear today *anywhere but in church.*

As I thought about this, I looked around and saw the familiar setting of the church sanctuary with new eyes and realized how anachronistic it was. Where today in our society do you find rows of straight-backed pews? Not in theatres, school auditoriums, nightclubs, stadiums, or living rooms. Where do you hear the language of the prayer book or of the old translations of the Bible? Only in church.

Even the illustrations used by the preacher that day in his finely structured sermon came from either geographical or chronological remoteness, unlike the illustrations from everyday life which Jesus used in His teaching and preaching.

Deep sadness settled over me, brought on by the painful awareness that most of our worship of Jesus Christ, the eternal contemporary and architect of the future, is archaic and identified with the past. The plain fact is that though the Incarnation, Crucifixion, and Resurrection are historical events, crucial to our authentic heritage, tradition, and message, the central figure in those events is not bound by them but is alive in the present and the future. And He is calling people forward now to new discoveries based on the fact of His life, death, and resurrection.

It may be that our whole emphasis on eschatology is wrong, and that we may be in the last days of "last days" thinking. Rather than living in the last days, we may be living in the initial stages of the Christian era. It is quite possible that God in His infinite love and patience has allowed mankind two thousand years in the laboratory of life to come up with a working blueprint or a few working models of "the new being" and "the new Jerusalem" that Christ made possible by His invasion of the world.

Perhaps we are not merely witnessing a great new reformation of the Church in our time, but the beginning of what God had in mind for man when He allowed the cosmic Christ to become the man Jesus twenty centuries ago. Maybe G. K. Chesterton was right when he said that Christianity has not been tried and found wanting; it has been found difficult and not tried. Or C. G. Jung may have hit on a profound truth when he spoke of Jesus Christ making possible a new rung on the ladder of evolution.

Whether renewal on such a grand scale is actually on God's timetable, there is nothing new about the concept of "the emerging Church." The true Church has always been the emerging Church in every age. That is to say, the real Church is always *about to be.* It does not look back to "the good old days" and it is not identified only with the past. It keeps hearing its Lord say to His faithful people, "I go before you . . ." even as He spoke those words to the first apostles who wanted to relive the past in Jerusalem.

To seek to recapture the glories of the past and return to the faith of our fathers is to assume that the Church was at one time all that God meant it to be. Well, it never was. Christ constantly calls His people forward to new commitment, new vision, and new forms. To be obedient to its Lord, the Church must be contemporary in its life style.

One of man's sins, even among believing Christians, is that he tends to be reactionary, glorifying the past and always looking over his shoulder.

(Let us learn from Lot's wife!) To be effective twentieth-century Christians we must not slavishly ape the styles and traditions of the past, but rather hear the great unchanging God say again, as He said to His faithful people almost three thousand years ago, "Behold, I am doing a new thing. The old is passed away. Do you not perceive it?"

There is a new Church emerging in our day. It has the same Lord at the center, who by His life, death, and resurrection offers hope. And it is made up of the same kinds of members. But there is a whole new life style emerging.

This new Church will not be unlike the Church of the first century. In his book, *The Reconstruction of the Church—On What Pattern?* the venerable E. Stanley Jones outlines an exciting model for the Church of the future, based on an interpretation of the first-century church at Antioch. It is in marked contrast to the kind of church we have experienced all too often in this century.

Let me share with you part of a letter I received from a woman whose husband is a leading elder in a very conservative West Coast church:

"My husband is a much-beloved church leader, praised and admired. Doctors tell me that he is psychotic, a very sick man. When you see the one you love so much turning bitterly hostile, drawing further and further away in a shell of loneliness, yet still teaching all the truth, there is a continuing grief that cannot be expressed.

"Every attempt at help is blocked. Every expression of love interpreted in the wrong way. And all the while his Christian friends admire and praise him and force him further and further into his prison of loneliness, where any admission of fault or failure becomes so threatening that it seems to mean destruction.

"This is the tragedy of the Christian community. We fawn and flatter and drown out the silent pleas for help from people until they cease to cry and lean on the praise for survival."

What an astonishing parallel this man's dilemma provides for much that is wrong in our church life today! It seems to me that sin, which is nothing more than disobedience to God, looks more like this kind of spiritual schizophrenia to which many of us have become accustomed than it does to the more blatant forms of secular rebellion. Instead of being the place where healing and wholeness ought to be known and expressed, the Church has become a place where people remain in their illness. And the institution therefore reflects on a large scale the impotence and sterility which are the marks of its individual members.

It is difficult to know just where we got off the track in the Church. Shall we lay the blame primarily on the clergy or on the laity? No doubt the blame may be shared equally.

In his book, *Inside the Third Reich**, Albert Speer, one of Adolf Hitler's inner circle, provides a remarkable description of Hitler. Here is what Speer says:

> I suppose if Adolf Hitler had ever had a friend, I would have been that friend. . . . Hitler could fascinate. He wallowed in his own charisma, but he could not respond to friendship. Instinctively he repelled it. The normal sympathies that normal men and women enjoy were just not in him. At the core in the place where the heart should be, Hitler was a hollow man. He was empty. We who were really close to him, or thought we were, all came to sense this, however slowly. You couldn't even enjoy eating cherries with him. We were all, all of us, simply projections of his gigantic ego. . . . And yet Adolf Hitler was my destiny. As long as he was alive he dominated my spirit, at least in part, and to the bitter end the man's drive—his iron will, his demonism—fascinated even while it repelled. Hitler *was* the Third Reich. All the rest of us were spearholders. . . .

I am intrigued and repelled by this description and my mind turns to other men and women of charisma, some of whom have used their gifts to speak about Jesus Christ, to inspire people, and to lead them to depths of commitment; but who are at the same time hollow, unrelatable, unable to give or receive love, unable to be friends or to have friends.

Perhaps this is the kind of thing the Apostle Paul had in mind when he wrote, "If I speak with the eloquence of men and of angels, but have no love, I become no more than blaring brass or crashing cymbal" (I Corinthians 13:1; Phillips).

It is love, vulnerable and affirmative, which is the genius of the whole Christian experiment. This is the mark of the new kind of society called "the Church" or "the Body of Christ" which God came into the world to create.

In this society, we are to experience relationships—and to become those who because Christ is in us can become relatable to others—in at least the four dimensions mentioned in this book. A glimpse of what the new Church might look like can be seen in a letter from a teen-ager

---

*Albert Speer, *Inside the Third Reich* (New York: The Macmillan Company). The passage quoted is from an article, "The Devil's Architect," by James P. O'Donnell, published in *The New York Times Magazine*, October 26, 1969.

whom I don't know personally, but who lives in the deep South. Here is what she says:

"My campaigners leader suggested that I write to you about the neat thing that happened to me last week. Jan asked us what one thing we wouldn't do without Christ in our lives. One of the many things I wouldn't do is tell my father I love him.

"I prayed that afternoon and that night and the next day at school that Christ would first give me the will to tell my father how much I love him and then to make me do it.

"My parents love me a great deal, and I love them, too. I have always been pretty close to my mother, but my father and I have always been distant. I felt as if he didn't think I loved him. Telling someone I love them is the hardest thing I have ever done, and I know it would be impossible without Christ. . . ."

She then goes on to tell about praying for the courage to go to her father and tell him what he had meant to her over the years. And one day she left school early and went to her father's office, just to tell him this one thing. There were tears and laughter and a new relationship between the two of them.

It seems to me that this is the kind of thing that the Church is all about. Because of the dynamic of Jesus Christ and His love for us, we become released to tell people how much they mean to us—to affirm them, to become vulnerable even with a parent or a spouse, let alone a stranger.

The group this young girl describes is a far cry from the old type of group that emphasized feeling "saved" in a doctrinal sense and then sent converts to start working on his family with the "I'm saved; are you?" type of approach.

Realizing that "orthodoxy" has more to do with relatability than with doctrine provides a turning point and opens a whole new style for our relationships as Christians in the Church and in the small groups that make up the Church. But I suspect that for us Americans, despite our gregariousness, true relatability poses real difficulties. We talk a lot about getting together, and when we get together we talk a lot, but is it dialogue in the best sense of the word?

When I think about dialogue, a picture flashes into my mind. It is an image which conveys to me the atmosphere in which true dialogue takes place. I was riding on a train from Cairo to Luxor. As I looked out the window, I caught sight of a little Egyptian village on the banks of the Nile. Kneeling on the riverbank, washing pots and pans, were four or five women, and standing knee-deep in the water, scrubbing his white horse, was a stark naked man. The man and the women seemed to be busily engaged in conversation.

This glimpse into the life of another culture, so different from ours, made me instantly wistful for the kind of experience it appeared to represent: the intimate sharing of everyday cares and concerns in a setting of unashamed openness. This is very difficult for us Americans, with our heritage of Victorian uptightness, for we tend to confuse intimacy with carnality and therefore rule out the whole thing.

When I characterize our culture this way, however, I am perhaps being unfair and am thinking primarily of that part of it in which I usually find myself: the world of the white, white collar, urban and suburban middle class. Certainly my experiences outside this insular world have given me glimpses of other ways and other possibilities.

For example, I can remember during the Viet Nam war years, disembarking from a plane at Corpus Christi, Texas, and finding a group of over a hundred people on hand to greet the plane. There was a band in uniform, as well. I was wondering if perhaps we had a celebrity on the plane who was being welcomed by this throng.

I soon noticed that the cargo handlers were removing a coffin from the plane. Then a uniformed noncommissioned officer appeared, escorting the coffin. I saw, then, that the crowd was a funeral entourage of friends and neighbors who had come to the airport to share the grief of a family of Mexican-Americans receiving their boy home from Vietnam. The atmosphere of that scene was one of sympathy and solidarity, and it struck me that I was being a witness to true community spirit—something rather rare in the circles in which I usually move.

I remember also being a guest in the home of a black family who live in a public housing project on the Lower East Side in New York City. During my four days with that family I saw a kind of communal living that was new to me. It was like what I imagine life to be in Tahiti and in some African cultures.

Children came and went in the apartment building and they were loved and disciplined without regard to "who they belonged to." The children seemed to belong to everyone. My host had left some money out on a table, and though dozens of children passed through his apartment while I was there, not one of them touched the money.

As I recall these experiences, I catch a vision of what the Church should be like in freedom and relatability. Too often, I am afraid, we have focused on the family as an exclusive, hermetically sealed unit that tries to make it on its own with God's help, when what God has in mind is that we share the joys and burdens of marriage and parenthood with a larger community so that we can minister one to another and receive the help and encouragement that God has for us in one another. I am thinking of the family of faith as well as the natural family.

Freedom and relatability are elusive qualities, at least for some of us. I am convinced, nevertheless, that they are essential marks of the emerging Church. Whether we can achieve them will depend in part on whether we can avoid letting the Church be polarized by a new distinction between the conceptual and the relational.

In the old days, the Church suffered a polarity between pietism and activism. Two rather distinct camps existed, one believing in a personal walk with Jesus Christ and the other in becoming involved in lifting humanity's burdens.

This polarity existed for a long time and dulled the Church's witness, even though perceptive Christians kept warning against it. Even the great fundamentalist, William Jennings Bryan, tried to bring about a unified approach. Writing in the *Omaha World-Herald* in 1896, he said:

"Preaching the word must cover a vast field. It is a mistake to suppose that the function of the pulpit is confined within the explanation of the plan of salvation. The Bible does not justify any such conclusion—that is, not for the new pulpit. Only about one-fifth of the writings of the apostles are devoted to the plan of salvation, and all the rest are instructions for man's conduct of life—how he shall live. Therefore, whatever touches the ethics of life in the world, directly, is the proper theme for the pulpit of today, and that, too, without reference, except incidentally to life hereafter. Moreover, it is the duty of the new pulpit to set in motion moral and reformatory forces that shall penetrate to the very center of practical politics or to the center of any other stronghold of political vice and misrule. The new pulpit should be in all sorts of current life, but not of it."*

The pietist/activist polarity is fading, fortunately, at least for the evangelical part of the Church, as more and more we realize that both emphases are crucial. But there is a danger, I believe, that a new polarity will take its place: the personal/conceptual distinction which I have just mentioned.

----

*Quoted by Paul S. Rees in *The Covenant Companion*.

In terms of the personal, this distinction centers around the principle of leading from weakness and affirming others, the very life style we have been talking about in this book. The new breed of Christian believes that there is no way you can speak about Jesus Christ evangelistically without also speaking about yourself honestly. It is impossible to present Jesus Christ in His perfection without giving people yourself in your imperfection.

This principle of the personal can also be seen in terms of social action. One can be involved in very impersonal programs to help society, or one can be involved quite vulnerably. Today the world is saying, "Don't give us more programs to help us. Give us yourself. Come and be among us, and together we may find a way out of our particular problems and dilemmas."

I firmly believe that it is a mark of the true Christian to be obedient to Jesus Christ by being personal both in his evangelistic work and in his social action, vulnerably and affirmatively relatable to those with whom he is in dialogue and to those whom he seeks to serve.

One of the prophets of this new day in the Church would certainly be Pope John XXIII, for he was a man who demonstrated this new style in a remarkable way. The response that the entire Church, both Protestant and Roman Catholic, made to him, and the response he received from the secular world and from other religious bodies, indicates the readiness of the world to hear this new breed of Christian.

What did Pope John do that was so unusual? Monsignor Robert J. Fox has helped us to understand the secret of this amazing man. Monsignor Fox describes Pope John as an old man in an age that worships youth; a fat man in an age that worships thinness; a man with a precarious power base in an age that worships power. In effect, Pope John threw open his purple and ermine robes and allowed the world to look at a simple peasant. Nothing was hidden: neither the layers of fat nor the plain and humorous face nor the lack of education nor the inelegance nor the earthiness. He let the world see John the man, and as such he became a spokesman for Jesus Christ. Though he was an interim pope, he captured the hearts and minds of the world and set in motion a new force in the Church that cannot be reversed. He related to the world as a man by being vulnerable, himself, and by affirming the potential in the world to respond to what he felt was God's imperative for our time.

The emerging Church will not be much concerned about religion. This is as it should be, for Jesus Himself didn't seem to care much for religion. He was constantly being attacked by the religious people of His day because of His attitude toward religious customs and traditions. In Jesus we see a great difference between "being religious" and knowing the Father and doing His will. Our relationship to God, made possible by Jesus Christ, and our relationships to one another become the focus and concern of the new Church. Religious trappings have had their day.

Some years ago I happened to be in England during a time when Parliament was having one of its perennial discussions about changing the Prayer Book. The Anglican Church, being the state church, must legislate any change through this parliamentary group. After a long debate, one of the members of the House of Commons stood up and said, "I want to go on record as being unalterably opposed to any change in the Book of Common Prayer. It's all that stands between us and Christianity."

Most change is perceived as loss and is therefore threatening and yet we need to challenge many of our forms so that we might be loyal to the Lord of the Church and recapture the basic orthodoxy of relationships by which we can measure truth, health, and authentic life in the Church.

The emerging Church will also realize, like Pope John XXIII, that part of the power of the Church is its freedom to be itself—to tell it like it is—to affirm the humanity of its various members while at the same time proclaiming the divinity of the Lord of the Church who is in us and with us.

Some years ago I attended a clergy conference that, for the first twenty-four hours, was nice and polite and full of treacle and unreality. Everyone was being ecumenical; everyone was preferring everyone else; and nothing of any significance was happening.

Then a Roman Catholic priest from New Orleans got up and spoke to the assembly. "Let me tell you a parable. When I was a boy, I lived on a dairy farm. My first job was to pick up the wheelbarrow and fork cow manure from the pasture and bring it to a pile in the barnyard.

"I hated that job; despised it. And then one day the word of the Lord came to me at a 4-H meeting. I discovered there that what I was picking up was not manure but fertilizer.

"Therefore, gentlemen, I have found that the things that are wrong in my life I have treated like manure, and hid them from public gaze— even hid them from my own eyes. But now I want to tell you what I am like, because I believe this is both fertilizer for my own growth and for a relationship that God can give us here in our churches."

As he went on to tell a bit about his own present struggles and growth,

I could sense the whole conference opening up. His struggles and short-comings became the fertilizer which stirred new growth by stimulating the rest of us to identify with him and reach out for God's help.

Before that conference ended two days later, Pentecost had come among us and the healing of Christ was evident. I have kept in touch with a number of men who attended that conference, and the new life that God gave us has continued in our personal lives, marriages, and churches. It began because one among us dared to believe that his human weakness was not manure to be hidden but fertilizer to be shared, compost to nurture the soil of the soul and promote spiritual growth.

How much we need to discover the good news in Jesus Christ that we are no longer strangers from God or from one another, but a society of people living out a style of life in openness in our relationship to God and each other, and sharing a ministry to the world that becomes the mark of this gospel incarnated in us!

STUDY GUIDE for No Longer Strangers

1: Relational Theology

1. Whether we realize it or not, we all have a basic theology—certain things we believe to be true about God and life. How would you summarize your basic theology in one, or at most two, sentences?
2. How does that basic belief affect your relationships right now? Try to be specific.
3. The author proposes four ways in which we can begin to live more relationally. We need to: identify, include, encourage and embrace. Can you describe a relationship in your life that needs improving right now? What are some ways in which you could 1) identify with the person? 2) include him/her? 3) encourage? 4) embrace?

2: Communication

1. This chapter speaks first of all about our communication with God. Can you describe a time when you felt you heard God speaking to you about something specific?
2. All prayer is communication with God and much of our communication consists of intercession for our own needs or the needs of others. Can you share a time when you felt one of those prayers was specifically answered?
3. Chapter 3 is largely about communicating our faith to others. Can you describe some of the ways in which you've attempted to do that? Was your communication effective?

4. Have you attempted any "communication by signal," as the author describes it, i.e., wearing a cross, carrying your Bible or something similar? Did that prompt any positive (or negative) responses?
5. How sensitive are you about picking up nonverbal signals from others?

3: The New Goal . . . A Christian Style

1. If the Christian style centers in affirmation and vulnerability, perhaps we could start practicing those attitudes with ourselves. Name three things you like about yourself.
2. Can you describe some areas of your life that represent some degree of failure—or at least need for improvement?
3. Is there someone in your life who needs affirming right now? Who is that person and what could you do to affirm him or her?
4. Being vulnerable involves admitting our mistakes, saying we're sorry, asking for forgiveness. Can you describe a time when you were able to do this?

4: You and Your God

1. When did you first come to an awareness of God as a person?
2. How have your ideas about God changed since then?
3. The author makes the point that our ideas about God often get confused with legalism and keeping rules. One illustration makes the point that we get God confused with some judge on a high bench. Are there some basic rules that you think God insists on?
   Try filling in this sentence: To be a Christian, one must (or must not)

4. In what area of your life do you need to trust God right now?

5: You and Your Inner Self

1. Pretend for a moment that instead of being human, you are an animal, fish or bird. Which particular animal, fish or bird would you want to be and why?
2. How do the characteristics of your "pretend identity" relate to your ideas about your inner self?
3. Many of our feelings about ourselves and our worth or lack of it have their roots in our early childhood experiences. Can you describe some of the messages you got about yourself from those around you (parents, siblings or others) in your growing-up years?
4. Imagine you are applying for some job you have always wanted to have. Write a paragraph about yourself giving your qualifications.

6: You and Your Significant Others

1. Can you recall a time of extreme loneliness in your life? What were the circumstances?
2. Describe a time in your life when you had a genuine sense of belonging, i.e., in a club, a Scout troop, a church, a neighborhood "gang," etc.
3. Who are the "significant others" in your life right now?
4. How could you begin to act out God's love to one or more of those people this very week?

7: You and the World

1. Are there any places where you are presently involved or where you would like to be involved in a ministry in the world (as opposed to church-related service and ministry)?
2. How did you get involved (if you are)?
3. What are some of the difficulties for you as a Christian as you minister in a more secular setting?
4. What are some of the rewards?

8: A New Church for a New Day

1. Assuming you are presently a member of a worshiping congregation, can you name at least three things you like about that church?
2. What would you like to see changed and why?
3. Do you feel that those Christians you worship with are, for the most part, "No Longer Strangers"?
4. How could you help this to happen more?